HIS SISTER

WRITTEN BY:
LAQSHAY ARORA

INTRODUCTION:

25TH MAY 2023

Hi, I'm Urvi Khurana, a 27-year-old lesbian woman with a really cool attitude. As a cool person, I don't really care about much. I do whatever I want, wherever I want. So, I'm not like my mom, Anjali Khurana, who's a super responsible and caring woman. I love her to bits, and I love her even more when she rescues me from my dad, Kamal Khurana. Now, the Hindi meaning of Kamal is lotus, but don't take his name too seriously. Unlike the lotus flower, he is neither soft nor lovely. He is very strict and disciplined, barely cracking a smile once a year. Honestly, he's the only one who scares me. Not only did he send me to an all-girls' school and college but he also made me fear he might ruin my love life. Did he though? That's the story I'm about to share – the love story of my life, which started 5 years ago when I was queer...

Just a heads up! The italicized text you see is basically what was going on in my head at that time. Like, it's what I was thinking, saying to myself, or asking myself.

CHAPTER 1: AM I MAYBE A LESBIAN?

25TH MAY 2018

So, this all began with me becoming the victim of an arranged engagement. Being a young queer woman, it was already tough as you don't even know if you're into chicks or dudes.

But here's the deal – lots of Indian parents don't care if their daughter is queer, lesbian, or whatever. They have this checklist: find a man through friends, newspaper ads, or websites, and check his pics, job, and location. Then come the calls, meetings, and interrogations with neighbors to make sure he's the real deal. After all that, they decide on the guy. As a formality, the daughter is told to meet him and say yes because, apparently, parents can't mess up finding the perfect man.

My dad did all that, and here I was, stuck with my folks and the parents of this fat arrogant dude, Raja Kukreja, in the midst of discussions about Raja and my marriage.

Let me introduce you to his parents in short. His dad was kind of cool, like my mom, and his mother was kind of boring and strict, like my dad. There are more of them, but let's talk about them later. So, my parents and his parents were sitting in his house, and Raja's cool dad, Sonujeet, started showing us the ad of their company, Just Chill, to basically show how unique and awesome they thought their company was.

Now, let me tell you about their stupid ad.

The ad began with some guests hanging around in a decorative room, gathered to celebrate the birthday party of a character played by Raja's dad. Suddenly, the bell rang. He opened the door and saw Raja.

Raja, in this scenario, was playing the character of his dad's close neighbor. He entered and said something so obvious. "Hello, uncle, happy birthday."

"Thanks, son, come inside."

As Raja entered the house, he noticed that despite the vibrant decorations, the guests weren't in a celebratory mood. The atmosphere was unusually quiet, and the guests seemed somewhat bored—almost as bored as you get when you're sitting next to Raja in real life. Raja curiously asked, "Uncle, what's happening? Why no music?"

His dad responded, "I'm not sure, son, but my speakers are not working."

Raja rolled his eyes and said, "What about your AC?"

Puzzled, his dad replied, "My AC?"

"Yeah, it's working fine. Right?" Raja asked.

Still pretty confused, his dad pondered, "It is, but what does my AC have to do with the speaker problem?"

Raja smirked, "Why not, uncle? When the AC can chill your room, then why can't it chill you too? Order Just Chill AC right now and feel the change. Just Chill AC doesn't just chill your room; it even plays your favorite music on demand. So, not just the room, you chill too."

His dad gave an amazed look and, with the excitement of a 10-year-old kid in front of an ice cream shop, said, "Son, order Just Chill AC for me and my family right now. It sounds so awesome; I want this in every one of my rooms."

After some hours with the Just Chill AC installed in the birthday party room, Raja said, "JC, play the Just Chill song." The Just Chill AC replied like Alexa, 'JC playing Just Chill song...' As soon as the hit song from the Salman Khan movie started playing, the guests inside began dancing like a couple of stupid, drunken fools who just won a big lottery.

And thankfully, this ad ended. But unfortunately, now they wanted our feedback, mostly mine. Although I wanted to call this ad stupid, crap, and a complete waste of my precious time, I couldn't because my dad was there.

Instead, I chose to ask them a question. "You know, you can play music on your phone or TV, so why specially order another AC just to play the music?"

Mark my words, but when I said that, there was a 20-second silence, with Raja and his parents looking at each other, thinking how to respond. Somehow, Raja's dad came up with a reply. "Actually, we forgot to mention in the ad that my character's TV was broken and the mobile's battery had died."

"What about the charger?" I questioned.

A loud voice echoed in the room as my dad shouted angrily, "Urvi!"

So, I stopped talking and my mother started. "Raja, tell us something about yourself. We believe you are the right guy for our Urvi."

"If you already think that I am the right guy for your daughter, then why should I say something about me to lose my chances?" Raja remarked, thinking that he had said something clever.

"Raja, stop joking around and tell them that you are the owner of our Just Chill AC brand." His dad insisted.

"But I am not. The company is registered in your name."

"Yes, but after my death, it will be yours, my son."

"I know, but the problem is that you are incredibly healthy. It will take way too long for it to be mine." Raja responded, looking sad.

Believe me, his remark made his dad fear for his life, and there was a huge silence. His mom, Kirti, glared at Raja and broke the silence, "Let's stop talking about death for a moment." Then she looked at me and added, "Urvi, please share a bit about yourself."

"I just completed my BA." I informed.

"What are your future plans?"

"Umm... thinking of doing an MBA, maybe."

"MBA, nice Urvi." Raja's dad remarked.

"Oh, MBA, so easy. I just completed that. Maybe I can teach you." Raja suggested, trying to impress me.

"But you still have some back papers to pass." His dad pointed out.

"They are easy, dad. I will pass them."

"You have been saying that for two years, boy."

"Yeah, Raja, I will definitely let you teach me." I replied sarcastically.

Suddenly, Raja's grandmother came in. She looked kind of angry and frustrated at something.

"Granny has come." Raja announced.

His dad looked at me and my parents and added, "Khuranas, this is our granny."

"What nonsense! What do you mean by saying our granny? I am just Raja and Isha's granny, not this house's."

You ever notice how first impressions can mess with you? Well, when Raja's dad introduced her as 'our granny', it got stuck in my mind, and I ended up calling her granny for so long, till she warned me not to.

"No, mother, I meant..."

"I don't want to hear any more of your stupid words. I have been insulted enough already." Granny interrupted. She then looked at me and my parents and asked, "Who are these people?"

"They have come to see Raja." Raja's mom replied.

"I have been hearing their voices for hours. Haven't they seen him already?"

"No, mom, they have come to see Raja for the marriage with their daughter, Urvi."

"Oh, okay. You all continue. I just know one thing: whenever a girl sees my handsome Raja, she just can't possibly reject him."

So, from the dialogue above, you get that his grandmother was quite the character, with a great sense of humor. 'Handsome Raja.' haha. It still makes me laugh as I write this. But let's move on.

"Mom, did you come here to say something?" Raja's dad inquired.

"Yes! That piece of garbage AC, what was its name? Joota sheel?"

"It's Just Chill AC, mom."

"Joota sheel." I couldn't help but laugh. "Urvi!" My dad shouted, as he often did.

"Anyway, that stupid AC is just playing music and not cooling my room. Throw it in the garbage where it belongs and get two fans for my room instead."

"Let me check." Raja's dad said. He looked a bit embarrassed as he got up and went with granny to check the AC.

Then Monu, their servant, walked into the room.

If you've ever worked in a company, you've likely come across someone who does absolutely nothing, yet, for some mysterious reason, never gets fired. They just keep on getting paid. Well, that's Monu for you. He was this lazy, good-for-nothing guy in his mid-thirties.

Wait, he's older than me, so maybe I should talk about him with some respect. Nah, that's not my style. He was a loser.

Anyways, what he did was when you ask him to do something, he would keep on asking you questions until you get fed up, get irritated, and finally end up doing the work yourself. You'll get it soon.

"This is our servant, Monu." Raja announced. Monu waved his hand. "Now, him we can say is our servant." Raja tried to joke, referring back to his granny getting mad at 'our granny.'

Yeah, all his jokes were awful. That's why Monu was Raja's only friend in the world, and even Monu made fun of him all the time, and he should have.

Monu came near Raja, and they both started talking in whispers.

"Has this girl come here to marry you?" Monu asked, talking about me.

"Yeah." Raja replied proudly.

"Do you really think that God created this beautiful girl to marry someone like you?"

"Don't talk nonsense, idiot." Raja retorted.

Raja’s mom pointed at Raja and Monu. "What are you boys whispering?"

"Nothing." Raja replied and then ordered Monu, "Go, Monu, bring us all a glass of juice."

"Which juice?" Monu asked.

"Apple."

"Which apple? Green or red?"

"Any."

"Should I make it or bring the one that is already in the fridge?"

"Make it."

"Green apple or red apple?"

"Monu, just leave. I will make it myself." Raja’s mom shouted angrily.

"So, what should I do with the juice in the fridge?"

"Monu, leave!" Raja’s mom ordered.

"As you say, madam." Monu replied and left.

"He is an old servant, so we have to bear with his tantrums. Although he does almost nothing here, the good part is he doesn't steal from us either." Raja revealed.

"Kamal, what's happening in your school? Is everything going fine?" Raja's mom asked. Then she added, "Being a principal must be tough."

"Yes."

"Is our daughter Isha doing well?"

"Yes."

Yeah, my dad wasn’t much of a talker unless he had to yell at me. Then he talked really for long. Anyways, Raja's dad came back.

"Is the AC working fine now?" Raja's mom asked curiously.

"It's working fine. Mom forgot to even switch it on. The music was playing on her phone."

Raja's dad then looked at my parents and asked, "What did I miss?"

"Not much, just discussing Raja and Urvi." My mom replied.

"How about this, let us leave these two alone for some time and let them get to know each other. Is it okay, Urvi?"

"Yes, Uncle." I replied as I prayed to God for my safety.

So, they all left, leaving us alone. We both sat in silence, and I didn't really know what to say to him. But unfortunately, he did. He came closer to me, and all I could think about was if there was a police station nearby.

You know, there are some people in our life, even if they haven't done anything wrong to us, just seeing them breathe makes you hate them, and that was Raja to me. Anyways, so he started talking.

"What's your hobby, Urvi?"

"I like listening to music."

"Oh, nice. Me too. Our AC plays music too."

There he goes with the promotion again. I am not here to buy an AC from you, dude!

"Yeah, I watched the ad." I replied.

"Do you want me to play that ad again?"

"No. God no!" I exclaimed, looking terrified.

"Oh, okay. Do you have a boyfriend?"

Could he be any more stupid? I was at his house for an arranged engagement. Of course, I didn’t have a boyfriend.

"No, I don't." I replied.

"Even I don't have a boyfriend." Raja said as he laughed at his own joke and then added, "Now tell me this. How many boyfriends have you had in your life? Tell me the total."

"I don't remember." I replied, as I controlled my anger. As a formality, I too asked him, "What about you? Do girls like you?"

"Me? Oh, girls are crazy for me. Every girl who sees me is like, Marry me, marry me, please." Raja replied proudly.

"Then why are you having an arranged marriage?"

"I am choosy."

"I am sure you are." I replied sarcastically.

It had been hours, and he was still talking and talking. *Someone, please make him stop. Please make him stop!* My ears were bleeding. Then he started showing his TikTok account and his awful dance moves. Then he showed me his Instagram reels. Then he started talking again.

"You know, my friends are always like, just marry someone, marry someone dude. In this difficult time, when a good man is hard to find, a girl needs a god-gifted man like you…"

I had no option but to fake a smile. Every second with him felt like hours. Every hour with him felt like days. Inside, I was crying and begging for forgiveness. *Where are my parents? Have they left me?* I was looking everywhere in the house, but they were nowhere to be seen. *Have they betrayed me? Am I in hell?*

"In my 10th class, one day I was looking for my vest, but I couldn't find it. So, I wore my mother's bra under my T-shirt. Blah blah blah." Raja said, as he continued his endless chatter.

I don't really remember all the torture coming out of his mouth, so the blah blah blah. So, after days or maybe years, my parents came to rescue me from this creep. Yeah, his parents were there too.

"Can we come back, or do you both want to talk some more?" His dad asked.

"Mom, please, let's go home." I replied, looking as if I was about to cry.

"What? Why?" My mom asked curiously.

Maybe I had said something wrong, as they all were staring at me eagerly, waiting for my reply.

"No, no, I meant, they all look busy. Let's not waste their time anymore and discuss the marriage some other time."

"We are completely free, Urvi. Don't worry." Raja's dad said.

"Do you like Raja?" Raja's mom asked as she stared at me.

"Umm... mom, dad, can I talk to you in private?" I requested.

"No. Whatever you want to say, say it in front of them. Be bold. Be strong. You can't hide from everyone all the time. It's a simple yes or no question… Do you like him or not?" My dad replied.

I was really nervous just because my parents were there; otherwise, I would have kicked Raja's big fat a*s. Having already said no to two guys that month, I was afraid my parents might even disown me if I said no again. The constant thought that came to my mind was maybe he'll say no and save my life.

"First, please ask Raja if he likes me." I replied.

"Raja?" His dad asked.

Raja looked at me, and I made the weirdest and most disgusting expression with my face in the hope of looking bad and getting rejected by him.

"I love her." Raja replied as he stared at me with his devilish eyes.

"So, are you okay with the marriage?" His dad asked again as I crossed my fingers.

"Absolutely, dad." Raja replied with a grin.

And he calls himself choosy, that lying bastard!

"Urvi, it's your turn now." His mom stated as she stared at me again.

To make it worse and even riskier for me to reject him, Monu and granny also came there. They were all eagerly waiting for my reply. I thought of faking a heart attack but realized it wouldn't work, as I was caught by my dad last time, and he got really mad at me.

"I..." I uttered as I thought of a polite way to reject him.

"Tell Urvi, we all are waiting." His mom interjected.

"Yeah, please say something." Monu said with a smile. He was sure that I would reject Raja, which made him really happy.

"Don't think too much, just say whatever you feel like." Raja's dad suggested, trying to calm me.

"We all know you will say yes, so just say it. Why say yes tomorrow when you can say it today?" Raja asserted, super confident as always.

That comment of his made me really angry, and I became sure to reject him, even if it meant my parents getting mad at me and throwing me out of their house.

"I really hate..."

So, I was about to complete the sentence by saying "this creep." but suddenly, Raja's sister, Isha, entered the house.

The moment I saw her, the word 'queer' got tossed out of my dictionary. She was wearing a beautiful black sari, her fair skin, dark brown eyes, and short, neatly combed hair made me go really crazy for her. Yeah, she seemed just a bit older and taller than me. Anyways, she looked flawless. *Does she go to school like that every day? Could she teach me something new? Wait, am I maybe a lesbian?*

CHAPTER 2: TEST MATCH

So, I was about to reject Raja when my lesbian turn-on button, Isha, entered the house.

"Mom, I'm home." She said.

She looked at all of us sitting together and got a little shy. "Oh, sorry, am I interrupting?"

"No, Isha." Raja's dad replied, as he stood up to introduce her. "This is Isha, our daughter and Raja's sister."

We all greeted her, and she politely greeted us back. I wondered how Raja and she could come out of the same woman.

"Isha, they've come to meet Raja. We were just finding out if Urvi likes Raja as much as we like her." Her dad explained.

"Oh!" Isha exclaimed.

"Yes, Urvi…. You were saying…" Raja's mom said.

Even though I would have loved rejecting Raja as much as any other girl, seeing Isha changed my mind, so I devised a plan to get closer to her.

"I meant, I really hate these kinds of situations. But I do like Raja." I said.

They laughed and clapped. Monu went to the bathroom, probably to vomit.

"I told you, dad! Girls go crazy for me." Raja bragged.

"Very good, my lion." His dad praised.

"But..." I said.

"But what?" Raja's mom asked.

"If you don't mind, I'd like to live here a month before making my final decision. I want to get to know this family so there are no regrets after marriage."

"What nonsense!" My dad yelled angrily.

"It's okay." Raja's dad said calmly.

Raja's mom agreed. My mother did too until my dad glared at her, and then she changed her mind.

"Urvi's right. Marriage is a big decision. A trial period could help her decide by the last day. She's welcome to stay." Raja's dad said gently.

"Thanks for understanding, Uncle." I said.

"Urvi, Anjali, come with me. Let's talk in private." My dad ordered, taking me and my mother aside.

Oh, really dad, now you want to talk privately. Be bold, be strong, don't hide from the world. What happened to all that?

"What is this nonsense? Do you even know who these people are? Who are you to embarrass us like this? First mocking their ad, now this. What's your problem?"

"Stop it! She's just a kid." My mom said.

"Teach her manners, Anjali, or I'll slap her right now."

"Dad, you've already chosen my school, my college, and this new guy. I just want to know my future family. If getting to know them is also wrong according to you, then just do it, dad, slap me. You will love it, right?"

My dad got even angrier as he raised his hand to slap me. But luckily, Monu came in with a plate full of samosas and green chutney, interrupting us.

"Do any of you want some samosas? They are super fresh, and the green chutney is yummy. It's good for your tummy." Monu said with a smile.

My dad was too angry at me to fully grasp his yummy tummy rhyme, but if he was a student who had said something like that in front of my dad, he would have beaten him left and right.

"I am waiting outside in the car. Anjali, you come with me. Some people have a 30-day test to finish."

So, my dad left, but my mother stayed for a bit to calm me.

"I didn't mean today, mom. I am not starting this 30-day thing right now."

"Yes, Urvi, I know. Don't worry. You know your dad very well. He will calm down. You can stay with us until you want."

"Thank God!" I exclaimed.

"You may start your test match from 1st June." My mom said jokingly.

"It's not a test match, mom. Can I go with you guys to home now?"

"No, stay here. Your dad is angry. Give me some time to calm him down. You discuss your living arrangement with them and book an Uber. We will see you at dinner. Okay?"

"Yes, mom."

My mom left, but Monu was still standing there, as he was busy watching our family drama.

"Did I come here at the wrong time?" Monu asked.

"You came at the best time possible. You saved me from getting slapped." I replied with a smile.

"On that occasion, eat a samosa?"

"Sure, bring me a plate."

"Which plate? Glass or plastic?"

"You don't do any work around here, right?"

"You know me now."

Back home, I had dinner with my parents. My mother managed to convince my dad, and he agreed to the arrangement. I promised to behave, focus on Raja, respect him and his family members, even though it was a bit of a LOL moment because, well, I'm not great with promises.

The next few days were filled with online and offline shopping, sneaking some clothes from my mother's closet—you know, the usual stuff. Finally, on my last night at home before the test match, it was past my bedtime, but I couldn't sleep. Thoughts of Isha filled my mind, even though I promised not to stalk her.

Unable to resist, I gave in to temptation and started stalking her like any other pervert. I turned on my phone and began scrolling through Facebook, searching for her name. *Where are you, Isha? Isha Kukreja? Come on, she's so difficult to find. Is she even on Facebook or not? These people make stalking really difficult.*

Suddenly, my mom entered my bedroom and asked, "Urvi, are you nervous for tomorrow?"

"Me? Nah, you know me. I don't take too much tension."

"Take some tension and please behave there."

"Yeah, yeah, don't worry, mom."

My mother was leaving, but she stopped, turned to me, and said, “"I still don't understand you.”

“What?"

"Are you really interested in marrying Raja?"

"Umm… hmm..." I replied.

She stared at me and added. "If you are, then say yes. You know you can't lie to me."

"I mean, he's fine."

"Oh, so what do you like about him?"

"I like his... curly hair."

"Come on, Urvi, stop lying to me. We both know what's going on."

"Then please tell me, mom, what do you think is going on?"

"You know you were about to reject Raja, and you changed your decision when you saw Isha."

"What? No. Who is Isha? I like dudes, mom."

"Oh really? Give me your phone."

"No, please, Mom, no."

My mom snatched my phone from my hand and saw Isha Kukreja on the Facebook search page. "I knew it. So, you started searching her online, huh? Couldn't even wait one day to meet her?"

"Come on, mom!"

My mom gave me my phone back. "You know I will support you no matter who you love, but at least stop lying to me, Urvi."

I held my mom tightly for a bit, and whispered, "Really, mom?"

"Yes, I just want you to be happy."

Tears filled my eyes as I confessed, "To tell you the truth, Mom, I don't even know who I'm attracted to. Being around the same gender so much since childhood has left me all confused."

"Don't worry, sweetie. You'll figure it out, and I'll always support you." She reassured me with love in her eyes.

"Love you, mom. I'll miss you there."

"Love you too, Urvi. But please do give Raja a chance!"

Suddenly, my dad's loud voice echoed, "Anjali, where are you? Don't you have to sleep?"

"Yes, yes, coming." My mom replied.

"Urvi, you sleep too. You have to wake up early tomorrow." My dad's voice again from his room.

"Okay, dad."

"What does 'early' mean in my dad's dictionary?" I asked my mom in fear.

"It means you'll be outside their house with your purse before their family members have even woken up."

"Nah, my dad isn't so bad; he won't do this to me. You're joking, right?"

The next day, at 6:30 am, I was standing outside the Kukreja's house, carrying a small purse. Yeah, my mom wasn't joking, my dad woke me up at 5, "Wake up, Urvi. Go early, the earlier you go, the more they'll be impressed." And after bathing and other nonsense stuff, I ended up here.

My dad had already sent my suitcase to them the day before so they could check for any dangerous items I might have brought. What did my dad think of me? Did he think of me as a terrorist? Anyways, I was feeling really sleepy as I had been watching memes and shorts until 2 am.

Let's ring the bell and see what happens. So, I rang the bell. "Someone, please open the door. I'm tired; I just wanna sleep."

After ringing like 2 or 3 times, I just gave up. I thought of sleeping outside their door but realized I was not a hobo, drunk, or a dog. I wanted to call my parents to inform them about this, but I checked and found that my phone battery had already died. Thanks, memers.

I looked up and saw the window of one of their rooms open and a drain pipe near it that was good enough to climb. *I don't think they'll be opening this door anytime soon. I might have to climb and enter through their window. No, I won't do it. I'm not a mad person. I mean, who in this world climbs through their future husband or future wife's window just to get into a room to sleep? Sleeping isn't that important.*

I yawned again, and within a few minutes, I found myself climbing through the pipe, nearing that window. *I hope they don't see me like this.* So, I reached the window somehow and saw that the room was fully empty, and most importantly, it had an AC. *It's empty, it's empty. I can finally sleep.* I threw my purse somewhere, switched on the AC, closed the door, and without a care in the world, I went to sleep.

After about 2 hours, I woke up, opened my eyes, and saw their whole family, other than granny and Isha, staring at me. They all looked confused. But at that time, I didn't know what to say to them. So, I said something that they probably should have said to me."Hmm, what's happening? What are you…doing here?" I said, still a bit sleepy.

I added, "Oh, sorry. You must be thinking of asking me the same question, right? Urvi, how did you come? We were all sleeping. Hahaha."

I stood up and said, "Anyways, I have to go to the bathroom." As I turned to leave, suddenly, someone held my hand to stop me.

Oh no, am I in trouble?

I turned around and saw it was Raja's mom.

"How did you enter the house and when?" She inquired.

"Oh, the thing is... Sonu opened the door at 7 AM."

"I?" Raja's dad questioned.

"Sonu? His name is Sonujeet; at least call him uncle." Raja's mom said angrily.

"No, no, sorry, I meant Monu."

"Monu, when did you start waking up this early? You never wake up without us slapping or screaming at you." Raja pointed out.

I looked at Monu, silently pleading with my hands, asking him to save me.

"Actually, I was in the bathroom, undrinking the water I drank last night. She rang the bell, I opened the door and welcomed her in."

"Seriously, undrinking it?" Raja asked.

"You want me to say pee in front of everyone?" Monu retorted angrily.

"Okay, okay, you both stop. Just forget that and make Urvi feel welcome in our home." Raja's dad intervened.

"Thanks, uncle." I expressed.

Raja came near to hug me. "Welcome, Urvi." He greeted, extending his arms. Ignoring the hug, I shook one of his big fat hands, and stated, "I'm not much of a hugger."

"Are you happy to see me?" He asked.

"No." I accidentally gave an honest reply, and they all stared at me.

"I meant not just you, Raja; I am happy to see all of you." I explained. They all smiled, and then Isha entered the room.

Approaching me, she greeted, "Welcome, Urvi." and extended her hand for a handshake, but I really wanted to hug her. Yeah, suddenly I became a hugger.

But I realized, no, not now. So, I just shook her beautiful soft hand. "Thanks. I'm really happy to meet you, Isha." I said.

"Me too." She responded with a beautiful smile, and then she left the room.

Then entered granny. *Can't they all come together so I don't have to greet them one by one?*

"Hi, Gran!"

"What's happening here? Who is she? What is gran? And why is this girl in my bedroom?" Granny asked angrily.

"Mom, this is Urvi. Remember, she came to see Raja for the marriage."

"Which one is she? The one we saw last week, last month, or the one we met in McDonald's?"

"Last week, last week, granny, stop!" Raja quickly interjected. And then he whispered, "Don't reveal too much."

"Okay, but so early she came. She must be really excited to meet you, Raja, right?" Granny commented.

"Yeah, granny, you know how girls go crazy for me." He replied.

I fake-smiled and was angry at my dad.

At 9:30 am, I walked down the stairs, heading to the kitchen for a quick snack. As I entered the living room, I noticed Raja and Isha talking while their dad was in his room, getting ready. I couldn't help but wonder what these siblings were discussing. *Are they talking about my thief-like entrance into their home*?

Anyways, I knew that the Just Chill company office was merely 10 minutes away, so that explained why Raja and his dad hadn't left for work. But what intrigued me more was why Isha hadn't left for school. *Has she taken a leave just to be with me?*

I entered the kitchen and saw Raja's mom there. "Hi, can I help you with something?" I offered.

"Sure, grate these carrots. I'm making carrot pudding." Raja's mom replied.

I was just being polite, and she actually gave me a chore. That's like offering money to a friend and them actually taking it. Pathetic!

She handed me a big bowl with over 10 carrots and a bat with so many holes in it; I guess it's called a grater.

"Grate it nicely; I am coming in a minute." She left without explaining how this carrot-grating thing worked and what this bat had to do with carrot pudding. Yeah, I didn't know how to cook except making Maggi. That too while watching a YouTube video on how to make it.

I was getting bored, so I decided to play cricket with these items. I used the grater as a bat and the carrot as a ball, and then I hit the carrot with the grater, and it flew and fell near Isha's feet.

Oh, what have I done! I quickly hid behind the fridge, but she had already seen me. She approached holding the carrot and remarked, "I found this."

"Sorry, it accidentally..."

She handed me the carrot and inquired, "What are you doing?"

"Grating carrot." I replied.

She stared at me suspiciously and was about to leave when I stopped her. "Hey, hey, wait. Do you know how to do this?"

Isha gave me an amused look and asked, "You don't know how to grate?"

I admitted, "Nope."

She took the grater and a carrot from the bowl and, placing a plate below it, started to grate the carrot, and said, "Watch me."

Oh! I am always watching you, girl.

I continued looking at her, not that carrot-grating nonsense, but she noticed.

"I mean, watch how I am grating the carrots." She subtly hinted at me to stop staring at her.

"Yeah, I am obviously watching that only." I quickly responded.

She grated one full carrot and said, "Now that's how you do it. Got it?"

"Yes, thanks a lot, Isha."

"Will you be able to do it?" She asked.

"Sure."

She was about to leave, but I stopped her again. *Why do I keep on disturbing her?*

"Hey, no school today?"

"There is. But your dad told me that I could come a few hours late as he requested me to unpack your stuff and show you your room."

"You didn't have to do that. I could have unpacked it."

"He thought you would…make a mess."

"Yeah, he's probably right."

Isha smiled and asked, "Should I take you to your new room now?"

I was about to say 'ABSOLUTELY YES'. But then her mom came there and said, "Don't worry, Isha, I will show her the room. You go, have your breakfast and get ready for school."

"Okay, mom." Isha replied and then left from there.

If she wasn't her mom, I would have said, 'that stupid bi***!'. But now, I won't comment.

"Haven't you finished grating the carrots yet?" Raja's mom asked.

"Oh no, I was learning." I replied.

"Learning? How to grate carrots?" She asked in shock.

"Yeah." I replied, and she glared at me, thinking of me as a spoiled child, so I had to change the subject. "Let me serve them breakfast." I suggested.

"Yeah, you do that, and then grate the rest."

I served the food to Isha, Raja, and their dad, who were sitting outside the kitchen. *Where the hell this Monu servant is?*

After that, I started grating the rest of the carrots, and Raja's mom was cooking rotis. So, we were standing in the kitchen doing our things. I was in a spot where I could see Isha clearly, and looking at her, I commented.

"You know, you cook so well. Your food can make anyone look so good."

Then I remembered Raja. *Well, not everyone.*

"Home food is the healthiest, Urvi, that's the reason I don't let my kids eat outside junk food."

Not even Raja? His stomach has more junk food than a Chinese food stall.

"Yeah." I looked at Isha's beautiful saree and commented, "This dress is looking so good. Which brand is that?"

"I don't know, a boy gifted it."

"Boyfriend?" I questioned.

"Yes."

"And you don't mind?"

"Why would I mind? Everyone has boyfriends."

"So open-minded you are. Boyfriends? Really? Any marriage proposals?"

"What? No! But we think you both will make the perfect couple." Raja's mom suggested.

Am I in heaven, or is she high?

"Really?" I blushed and in excitement, added, "Can we marry?"

"What are you talking about, Urvi? That's why you came here, right? To tell us if you are interested in marrying Raja or not?" She replied angrily.

"Raja?"

I came near her and realized that from where Raja's mom was standing, she could only see Raja, so she was thinking that I was talking about Raja and not Isha.

"Oh, you were talking about Raja…" I said. She glared at me, wondering who I was talking about.

"I was joking, don't mind." I added, trying to cover this topic, filled with extreme embarrassment. In anger, she even gave me more carrots to grate.

CHAPTER 3: RAJA THE TIKTOKER

First, Isha left for school. Afterward, Raja and his dad got ready to leave too. Raja's mom and I stood near the door to say goodbye to them.

"Okay, so I have to go now. I will meet you in the evening." Raja said to me, looking emotional.

"Alright."

“If you get bored, call me." He added.

Why, fatty, to get even more bored?

"Sure." I replied.

"I will try to come as early as possible." He said.

Don't even think about it, loser!

"Okay, bye." I said, trying to make him leave.

"Take care and goodbye to both of you.” His dad said, and finally, they both left.

Raja's mom went to her room, probably to fulfill her addiction of watching TV serials.

Then, granny approached me and said, "Isha? Isha darling?"

"What? No, I'm Urvi…I wish I was Isha." I replied.

"Oh, sorry. You both look so similar." Granny remarked.

"Really?" I blushed and added.”Anything you want help with, my favourite granny?"

She gave me a medicine prescription paper and requested "I want these medicines."

I checked the prescription, and there were about 10 medicines.

"So many? Are you taking them all?" I asked.

"Yes, the doctor told me to take these, so I am taking them. Who cares?"

"Who cares? ... are you serious?"

She came near me and said, "Bring me a sweet too. Jalebi or Rasgulla, will do it."

"Sweet? Why?" I asked in surprise.

"After taking all these sore, filthy drugs, I need a sweet." She insisted.

"Okay, okay, I will bring them."

"God bless you." She said and left from there.

I was leaving for the market when Raja's mom came there to stop me. "Urvi, have you taken a bath? There is a towel in the bathroom. Please go!"

"No, no, I have to bring medicines for Raja's granny first." I responded quickly, looking like a cat afraid of baths, and left.

I went to the market and bought the medicines and sweets combo for granny. What a weird combination, right? Soon I gave them to her and listened to some Taylor Swift songs on spotify before going to sleep.

In the evening, Isha came home from school. As she entered, she said, "Mom, I'm home." My eyes automatically opened. I jumped out of my bed and hurried to Isha's room without even thinking about what to say to her.

She was unpacking her stuff when I entered her room, looking as happy as a dog when its owner comes home late from work. But when she looked at me, I didn't know what to say and got really nervous.

You know that feeling when you really like someone and want to impress them? You end up getting all weird and dumb around them. That's what happened.

"Hi, you came?" I awkwardly asked.

"Yeah." She replied, looking at me with an obvious expression.

"Umm, I can see you, right? So, you obviously have come. You came, that's so nice, right?" I babbled nervously.

She stared at me, looking confused.

"So, how was school?" I asked.

"It was good."

"Yeah, school is awesome. Did you teach the students?"

"I am a teacher, so yes."

WTF am I saying? I need to change the topic before she kicks me out of her room.

"Should I bring you something? Coke, water, tea, coffee, chips or anything? You must be tired." I offered like a street hawker.

"No, nothing for now. Thanks."

"Let me bring water at least." I insisted.

I left the room to go to the kitchen, and I'm pretty sure she rolled her eyes, thinking I was being silly. Within a few minutes, I returned with a plate and a glass full of water. As I approached her to hand over the glass, my nerves got the better of me. *Damn, she's so gorgeous.*

Consequently, I got all confused and extended my right hand, giving Isha an empty plate while holding the glass in my left hand. Realizing the silly mistake, I thought the next time I go to the chemist's shop, I should probably bring more medicines for me than for granny.

"Oh, sorry." I said as I handed her the glass of water, and she took it, saying thanks and returned it empty after drinking. *I knew it; she was thirsty.*

I was about to place the glass on the plate to take it back to the kitchen when she casually mentioned, "I am going to take a bath." Hearing that, the glass slipped out of my hand and shattered.

"Oops, sorry!"

"Are you all right?" She asked.

"Yeah, yeah, I'm fine. It happened by mistake. Let me clean it."

"No, no, it's okay. Monu will do it. You go and rest"

"I'm really, really sorry, Isha." I apologized again.

"Don't worry, Urvi. It happens…. I'm going to bathe now."

"Didn't you take a bath in the morning?".

"I did, and I do it in the evening too. It's a habit I've maintained since I was a kid. It freshens me."

"We both are so similar. I bathe at least twice in the day too."

Suddenly, her mother's loud voice echoed, "Urvi, where are you? Since morning I have been telling you to bathe. It's evening now. When will you bathe?"

Listening to that, Isha stared at me. I smiled and left with embarrassment. *Shit, all my chances with her seem to be gone now.*

At 8 p.m., we were all having dinner together at a big round table when Raja's dad asked me, "So, how was your day, Urvi?"

"It was good."

"Did you get bored?"

"No, she didn't. Otherwise, she would have called me." Raja said.

"Yeah."

"You have my phone number, right?" Raja inquired.

"I do."

"It's even written on the Just Chill AC in your room. So, even if you lose it, you will find it there."

"Thanks for writing your number on the AC." I said sarcastically.

"Do you sing songs, Urvi?" Raja's dad asked.

"I haven't tried yet."

"No worries, I will teach you. Let's do some karaoke after dinner." He suggested.

"Umm... hmm..."

"What? No! She is not here to become a singer. She has come here for Raja. Let them spend some time together… Urvi, you go for a long walk with him after dinner, okay?" Raja's mom said.

First of all, I came here for Isha, who probably hates me by now. Secondly, can this chatty fatty even do a long walk?

"Sure, I'll go for the walk." Then I added, "Isha, would you like to join us?" Suddenly, they all stared at me.

Why do they stare at me so much?

"No, no, I meant let's all go for a walk, right?"

"Don't be shy, Urvi. I know you think of me as this big VIP-type wealthy guy, but I'm just a common person like you, and a really fun guy to hang out with. Just get to know me properly, and I'm sure you'll be addicted to me in no time. And no pill will get rid of this addiction." Raja declared with a smile.

If there was a washroom or a pot nearby, I would have vomited after hearing what he said. I faked a smile because I didn't have any other option, but in my head, I was crying and thinking, *Please don't leave me alone with this creep at night.*

Late at night, I found myself in a peaceful place with beautiful trees and a great view. Shiny stars lit up the romantic sky, yet there I was, walking with Raja. Yeah, it sucked to me.

"So, I was thinking of launching the Just Chill cooler for poor people." Raja said as he broke the peaceful silence.

"Oh, okay."

"But I'm not sure where to put the speakers in the cooler. Or maybe we will put FM radio in it. What do you think?"

"Yeah, I would love to hear FM or music in my cooler when it's already making so much noise." I said sarcastically

"Right? It will be so cool. But not just the room, you chill too." He said, laughing at his own joke.

So, he kept on shooting these types of PJs in my ears. And when the whole place started stinking with bad jokes, he thought to ruin the vibe completely by talking about his TikTok account.

"Are you on TikTok?"

"No, I don't like it at all."

"Wait, you will start liking it soon, let me show you my account." He showed me just 2 of his TikTok videos, and they were enough to cause depression and anxiety inside me.

In the first one, he was dressed up in his white vest, wearing a red-coloured hair wig and dancing on the top of a Just Chill air conditioner with classic Bollywood music playing in the background. The video was cut short probably because his weight had caused the AC to shatter in pieces.

In the second video, there was a rope, but it wasn't a regular one. Raja had combined his mother's bras, around 5-6 of them, into a makeshift rope. Raja and Monu were playing tug of war with it, and the winner was promised a Just Chill air conditioner. In the end, Raja emerged as the winner and won the Just Chill AC as a prize.

Raja was about to show me the third TikTok video, but I told him that I was not ready to have so much fun at once.

"Did you like my channel?"

"All I can say is that your channel is just like you."

"Really? You liked it that much?"

After some distance, his legs probably got all confused, and wondered why this fat guy was suddenly using them. So, he kind of was about to trip when he somehow got hold of himself and said, "Urvi, you must be tired. Let's go home."

"Yes, please. I am really tired."

"Let me call the driver. I think we have gone too far, right?"

Absolutely, Raja. We might have walked to a different country. I think you should probably call your private plane to pick us up.

"Yeah, I think we are lost." I said sarcastically.

So, he called the driver and said to me, "Don't worry, the driver will find us. Till then, wanna eat something? I am really hungry."

"We are doing an after-dinner walk..."

"Hmm, you're right. Why not make a quick TikTok before the driver gets here?"

"Nah, your audience wants to see more of you."

"You're probably right. This dress of yours won't look good on my TikTok account anyways. My followers might hate it and unsubscribe from my channel."

I should've brought a knife with me.

At night, as I slept alone in my bedroom, I had a dream. In it, Isha and I were standing at a big wedding hall, both of us wearing Indian bridal dresses with veils covering our heads. Our family members were sitting in various seats nearby. And it was time for me to remove her veil that was fully covering her face, but as I did, I saw the deadliest thing. The face was of Raja. Seeing Raja next to me in the wedding hall in Isha's body, wearing an Indian bride dress, caused the shit out of my nightmares. I screamed as loudly as humanly possible.

He put a finger on my lips, telling me to calm down and said, "Why are you shouting, Urvi? This dress will look good on my TikTok channel. Let's make a video now."

I screamed aloud, woke up and saw Raja standing next to my bed, saying, "Hey, is everything all right?"

"I had a really bad dream."

"Don't worry, it's all fine now."

But it wasn't, as Raja brought two of his mother's bras from another room and asked me, "Which one do you think will look nice on me for my next TikTok video?"

"What?"

Suddenly, Monu came there wearing a pink blouse of Raja's mom. "Let's do it. Start the TikTok, guys."

I screamed again and realized that it was yet another nightmare. Maybe these are the dreams you get after walking with Raja.

Finally, I woke up and saw Monu standing next to my bed.

"What happened? ... Why are you screaming in your sleep again and again?" Monu asked curiously.

"Where’s the pink blouse that you were wearing of Raja's mom?"

"What?? Why would... what? Why would I wear a blouse?"

"Am I finally awake?"

"Yeah."

"You are not making a TikTok video, right?"

"No, who makes TikTok in the morning?"

"What time is it, Monu?"

"It's 11 am."

"11 am? Why didn't you wake me up?"

"Because I am not a chicken, that's why I didn't wake you up. Also, you don’t do anything around here so there’s no point in waking you up." Monu said jokingly and left from there.

"Ass****."

CHAPTER 4: LADY CHEATER

Following in Isha's footsteps, I started the new day with a morning bath, a rare occurrence for me. After that, I brushed my teeth and wore a lovely red dress, a gift from my mom on my last birthday. Then, I checked what Raja's mom was up to; she was, as usual, engrossed in an Indian family drama TV show in the living room.

"Hey, good morning."

"Morning."

"Don't you get bored being alone at home all day?"

"No, because I am never really alone."

"Yeah, but how long can you talk with Monu?"

She glared at me and clarified, "I wasn't talking about Monu."

She pointed at the television, "As long as I have shows like these, I'll never be lonely."

"What's this show's name?" I asked.

"It's Lady Cheater."

"Lady Cheater? That's a unique name. What's the story?"

"It's really interesting. You see, there's this girl Priya, and her parents arranged her marriage with a guy named Sahil. But after the wedding, she realized that Sahil was too mean and rude. So, she ends up falling for Sahil's brother Kapil, who is really caring and loving. There's this romantic tension going on between them."

I was shocked. *WTF! They made a show similar to my real-life story.*

"Oh, actually, I don't watch shows in which girls cheat." I said, trying to look innocent.

"These are not reality shows. Are you not interested if she will ever marry Kapil?"

"I'm not sure."

Obviously, yes. I will secretly watch this show every day. Maybe this show will give me some pointers on how to impress Isha.

"Raja called me to say that he'll come late today. He wanted to say goodbye to you, but you were sleeping."

"Oh really?"

"You must be sad that you're not able to spend more time with him."

"Hmm." I replied.

"Don't worry. Tomorrow is Sunday, so he will be there with you. Also, tomorrow is his cousin Suhani's wedding. We all are invited."

"Yeah, mom told me about that invitation."

Then, in the Lady Cheater show, a scene unfolded where Priya was washing clothes with her maid, and the maid said, "You know, I found something suspicious while cleaning Kapil's room."

"I don't want to know."

"Madam, all I can say is that there is a secret in every room."

"What did she find?" I shouted loudly.

"Shhh..." His mom said to calm me down.

I really wanted to know what she found in Kapil's room. But instead of wasting another 10-15 minutes on that, I thought, *why not check what was in Isha's room?* So, within a few minutes, I found myself snooping around in Isha's bedroom.

Let's spy the shit out of this room. I looked around and realized that the room was super clean, with everything neatly arranged. I started looking at her stuff and found something amazing: Yeah, Oreos and Nachos!

Now, this is the perfect girl to marry. Then, I saw a really cool rocking chair. *Am I in a hotel room or what?* While munching on the Doritos, I found a photo album containing some old pictures of Isha and her family members and noticed something strange. There were lots of photos of Isha with a guy who seemed like a family member, but something felt off.

Does Isha have another brother?

He didn't look like her brother. Despite being similar in height, not that it matters, but their skin colors differed significantly.

As I continued flipping through the photo album, I discovered something that shattered my dreams of being with Isha. There was a picture of that man kissing Isha on her cheeks, and it didn’t seem like a brotherly kiss.

Is Isha cheating on me? I wondered before realizing she wasn't even in a relationship with me.

Yeah, so he is definitely not her brother. But who is this guy? Who is this dog?

Suddenly, I heard Monu calling for me. "Urvi, madam, where are you?" I panicked, looking for a hiding spot in her room as I set down the photo album.

Before I could hide, Monu entered Isha's room and questioned, "Urvi, madam, what are you doing in Isha sister's bedroom?" I hastily replied, "Oh, I... Is this Isha's room? Oh, shoot, I didn't know."

"No problem. You are a guest here. It's okay."

"Why were you calling me, though?"

"Sorry, I forgot to tell you, Kirti Madam is looking for you."

I smiled and replied, "Okay, I am going to her. And you don't have to say sorry to me."

Suddenly, I noticed the look in his eyes, and it seemed like Monu was fantasizing about marrying me or something else. I decided to play along and said in a flirtatious voice, "And also, no Urvi Madam, never say Urvi Madam." He seemed really happy, probably thinking that cool girls find servants attractive.

"So, what should I say to you? Tell me, I will say that, please tell me something." He said in extreme excitement.

"Sister. You call Isha Sister, then why don't you say Urvi sister? You have to say that from now. Understood?"

His heart broke, and he ran away without saying a word. As a bad girl, all I did was laugh.

But as advertised or as they say, karma is a b****. I forgot that it wasn't my room as I tossed the half-eaten Doritos somewhere, fully messing up her arrangement, and went to see Raja's mom.

After a few hours, I was lying in my bed, on a call with my friend Sheila, and we were talking and laughing. "Yeah, those dreams really freaked me out…" While I was talking with her, Isha came inside the house with her usual, "Mom, I am home." I heard her voice and said to my friend on the call, "Isha has come. Yeah, I am telling you, Sheila. She is like the sweetest person on earth. Her voice is so sweet and calm." Suddenly, a loud voice echoed. Surprisingly, it was Isha's.

The reason was when she entered her bedroom and saw it all messed up with half-eaten nachos, the rocking chair, and the photo album in a different position, she got really angry and shouted, "Who touched my stuff?" I and Monu rushed to her room to see this new Angry Isha. As I entered, I realized the mess I made while spying, but acting innocent, I asked her, "What happened, Isha?"

"My room wasn't like this before."

I was really angry at myself for ruining Isha's mood after work, but I didn't know what to say. "Tell me, guys, who did it?" Isha asked. So, I thought to just tell the truth and get it over with. "Isha, actually..." I was about to confess, when Monu took all the blame and said, "Sorry, sister, I did it."

"You?" Isha stared at him.

"Yeah, it happened by mistake."

"Oh, really! So, by mistake, you ate my chips, and…"

"Actually, those were nachos." I interrupted, and she stared at me.

"Sorry." I apologized.

"Come on, sister, I was feeling munchy, so I sat on your rocking chair and ate your nachos. Oh, they were so crunchy." Monu said with a smile and added, "I was rocking it!"

"It's not a time for jokes, Monu. Everything is not a joke. We pay you for food, right?"

"Sorry, sister."

"Do we pay you to clean the room or mess it up?" Isha asked angrily. Monu stayed quiet, waiting for this drama to be over.

"Answer me!" Isha shouted. Her shout made him so nervous that he said, "Mess it up. No, sorry. Clean, to clean the room."

"It's your last warning; I am telling you." Isha warned him.

"Sorry, sister."

"Don't worry, Isha. I will teach him some manners." I reassured her, and Monu glared at me.

"It’s okay." Isha replied, controlling her anger. So, we both left her room, and I said to him, "Thanks a lot, Monu, for saving me."

"You’re welcome, Urvi madam”

“Urvi sister.” I said.

Monu smiled, thinking I was joking.

"I am not joking. Say, Urvi, sister!" I insisted. But he cried and ran from there. *Why doesn't he say it?*

At night, I entered Isha's room, and this time, she was inside, engrossed in a novel, wearing her reading glasses. " Hey, you're still awake?" Isha asked.

I smiled and replied, "It's just 9 pm, Isha. There have been days when I woke up at this time.” I added with a wink. She stared at me, and I quickly corrected myself, "Sorry, what I wanted to say was, I have to go outside for something important."

"Okay, be safe."

“Thanks, but I don't want to go alone. Actually, your mom said no. Your dad and brother are still tied up at the office. Your granny doesn't feel safe as there are too many perverts and drunks hanging out this time. And I don't feel safe with a character like Monu. You know, he still avoids calling me sister.”

"Hey, hey, it's okay. You didn't have to explain all that. You could have simply asked me to go with you." Isha reassured.

“Will you go with me?”

"Sure."

“Thanks a lot.”

“Let me change my dress."

I stood there in her room and nodded, "Yes, do it." She stared at me and said, "I meant alone."

"Yeah, obviously. I am waiting outside." I replied with embarrassment. *Why do I keep acting like a pervert in front of her?*

So, we both were walking in the night, it had been minutes, and I wasn't sure what to say or how to start. I wanted to ask her so many questions like, 'Who was that cheek-kisser photo album guy?', 'Are you straight?', 'Is Raja your real brother?' But I didn't know which one to ask her first.

Before I could ask her any, surprisingly, she broke the silence and asked, "By the way, what do you want to do?"

"Oh, me? Well, I'm thinking of becoming a fashion designer..."

"No, I meant where are we going?"

"Sorry, to the printout shop"

"Okay, the shop is nearby."

"Yeah, anyways, until we reach, tell me something about yourself. I don't really know much about you."

"Umm…my name is Isha."

"Yeah, okay. That's the most I know about you."

"That's not true. You also know that I am a teacher, right?"

"Yes, but I want to know more."

"Hmm, let me think."

"Please think. Something like a boyfriend or..."

"Okay, we have reached." She said as she showed me the shop and then added "Maybe next time I will tell you about myself."

"Well played. Why next time? We will be going back together, right?"

“Sure. Should we go inside?”

“No, you wait here. I am coming in a minute.”

I entered the shop, and the door automatically closed behind me. Then I took my selfie and said to the stationary guy, “Hey, I need a printout.”

“Sure. Mail me please.” He replied, showing me a small piece of paper stuck on the wall behind him with his mail ID written on it.

I emailed him my selfie and said, “You must have got it by now. Check.”

He saw the mail and asked.” You want a print out of your selfie?”

“Yeah, just do it.”

“Did you click it here?"

"Yes."

"By the way, you look really pretty in this.”

“Focus on the printing, not the picture.”

“I am trying.” He said with a smile.

I glared at him, and he gave me the printout instantly.

“Delete my selfie and tell me the price.”

“Here's a deal, you let me keep your selfie, I will pay you 10 rupees. If I delete, then you have to pay me 10 rupees.” He offered.

“What kind of pervert are you? Let me call the police.” I replied as I opened my purse and checked for my phone but I didn't bring it, and there were just bills and napkins in my purse. I may be in excitement of going with Isha, forgot to bring the money.

“Sorry, please don't call the police.” He requested.

“Don't worry, keep the selfie.” I said, calming him down.

"Really? … thanks." He said, looking surprised.

"Not thanks, give me the 10 rupees."

The guy gave me 10 rupees for keeping my selfie, and I just realized that this might be the cheapest thing I've done in my life, selling my selfie just for 10 rupees. Anyways, I happily put the selfie printout and the 10 rupees note in my purse and left this creep's shop.

"Did you get it?" Isha asked.

"Yup."

We were going back home, and she asked me, "If you don't mind, what was the important thing you wanted to print out so late at night?"

"It's personal stuff. Anyways, you were telling me about yourself."

"It's personal stuff." She replied jokingly.

"Come on, tell me something, girl. Are you an introvert?" I asked.

"Yes, maybe."

"Okay, let me start. After that, you will go. Deal?"

"Sure."

"Hmm. Where do I begin? So, people have been calling me Urvi for, like, the past 22 years. But I'm hoping to be seen as this big future fashion designer, which is what I want to become. Actually, it was my mother's dream, but her parents didn't allow it. I've decided that I will try my best to be that. You see, I have been secretly filling out these diploma forms for fashion designing because my dad probably won't like it. I am really scared of him, you know. He wants me to do an MBA, and if I disagree, he will probably scream, shout, and get even more embarrassed of me."

Suddenly, I saw Isha's face; she looked as if she felt sorry for me or something. I apologized to her and said, "Sorry, I made it all a bit too tense. Didn’t I? Yeah, I'm just a little bit talkative, and I love hanging out with good-hearted people like you.”

“I didn't know that you are talkative because Raja told me that you talk hardly talk.” Isha said.

"Oh yeah, it depends on my mood. Anyways, it's your turn now.” I replied.

“I don't know what to say. You tell me, what do you want to know about me?”

“Do you have a boyfriend?”

“No, I am not interested in that.”

“Are you not interested in boys or relationships?”

“To be honest, I am mar..." She was about to complete the sentence when suddenly a masked man approached us with a gun in his hand.

"Stop, both of you!" He said. We both stopped as he pointed his gun at us. "Give me your money.” He ordered.

"We don't have any.” I said.

"Stop lying, give it or I will shoot you both."

I handed the thief the 10 rupees note I got for selling my selfie, but it only seemed to infuriate him more. "10 rupees? Do you think I became a thief just to earn 10 rupees?" He asked angrily.

"It was your career choice..." I retorted.

"Don't make me mad, give me the money or I will shoot you both right now.” He threatened.

"But we really don't have any.” Isha replied in fear.

"What about gold or any expensive jewellery?" He asked.

"We are not running a cash-for-gold shop here, dude.” I joked.

"Don't joke. If you don't have money or gold, then you both have to dance together."

"Dance? Why?" Isha replied, looking shy.

"What kind of theft is that?" I questioned.

"I am the thief, so I will be the one who will decide. So now dance, or I will shoot you both." He shouted angrily.

"Ok, ok, we are dancing." I said.

I held Isha's hand, and we danced for about 20 seconds. OMG, I really loved that dance. It was just amazing. *More thieves should give these options to victims.*

But then he said, "Now kiss each other."

"What? No, this is too much." Isha exclaimed angrily.

"I don't want to get shot." I expressed as I came closer to Isha.

"Wait, let me check my purse." She stated, opening her purse, in it there was a secret pocket. From there, she pulled out four notes of 500 rupees and gave them to the thief and added, "Happy now? Take it and please leave us alone." The thief took the money and happily said, "Bye" before leaving.

I laughed and remarked, "Bye? What a ridiculous thief."

Isha smiled, and I asked her, "I thought you didn't have any money?"

"Actually, I saved this 2000 rupees for Suhani's marriage tomorrow. I wanted to give it to her as a wedding gift."

"Oh, I am really sorry." I expressed, looking sad.

"It's okay, I will think of some other gift."

"Sorry, one walk with me made your entire purse empty."

"Actually, it's not completely empty." She clarified as she opened her purse and took out my earrings that must have fallen when I was snooping in her bedroom.

She gave it to me and continued, "I found this in my room."

“I didn't know that Monu wears earrings nowadays." I replied.

She stared at me, and I quickly apologized, "Okay, okay, I'm sorry. I won't go to your room again."

"You can, but don't mess it up, please."

"Well, that's my style. Messing up is my style."

She smiled, and we realized that we had reached home.

I intentionally untied my shoelaces and told her, "You go, let me tie my shoelaces."

“You need privacy in that?" She asked.

"Yeah." She smiled and entered the house. I closed the door from outside, and then I walked some distance and found my fake thief there. He removed his mask. Yeah, it was my bestie, Sheila's brother, Sajal.

“Nice job!... now give me that 2,000 rupees.” I said and then snatched the money out of his hand.

"But you paid me only 500 rupees for this… At least give me another 500."

"I am not keeping this. I will give it to her in some other way. Now go before someone sees me with you."

And then the fake thief left. Yeah, it was all planned. This entire walk and printout nonsense was just to get that dance and, well, a kiss, which unfortunately couldn’t happen. Actually, when I was in her room to invite her to this, I snooped into her purse. I thought it was empty as I didn’t notice that secret pocket. So, I expected a lot, but still, at least I achieved something, right?

But what was she saying to me before the thief's entry? Is she married? Is that photo album guy her husband?

I was about to enter the house when Raja covered my eyes with his big fat palms and asked, "Guess who?”

These big palms suggest to me that you can either be an elephant or Raja.

“Raja?" I asked

"Oh, you guessed it right. Are you happy to see me?"

"I am happy." I replied.

Yeah, I was really happy after that dance with Isha. That I didn't even want to punch Raja for putting his dirty palms on my face.

"What did you make for dinner?" He asked.

"Why would I make dinner for you? We are not even married yet.”

We both entered the house, and Raja asked me, "By the way, who was that thief-looking guy outside?"

CHAPTER 5: THE PHOTO ALBUM GUY

The next day was exciting as it was the wedding day of Raja's cousin, Suhani. So, we were all getting ready. Surprisingly, granny was the most excited one for this wedding. She was in her bedroom, wearing a beautiful red suit, standing in front of a mirror, and grooming herself with the help of Monu. He was wearing a sports shirt, perhaps obtained from winning a cricket match in a nearby park.

There were all sorts of, should I say, decorative items for granny like bindis, flowers, clips, mobile covers, and tikas of different colors. Monu was giving them to granny one by one. She decided to go all red for the wedding, with a red bindi on her forehead, a red flower in her hair, red clips holding some of her hair, and a red cover for her mobile. After that, when she asked Monu for a black tika, Monu got all confused.

"Why not a red tika? I thought you were going there looking like a red light or something."

"Don't be a fool; it's for warding off the evil eye."

She put a black tika on the left side of her forehead and looked beautiful for her age.

Raja's dad, mom, and I were dressed up, and waiting for Raja and his sister Isha in the living room. Not to be a narcissist like Raja, but I was looking really pretty in that black saree. Anyways, Raja's mom was getting furious because they weren't coming on time. She said, "Isha, Raja, come on, hurry up, we are getting late, guys."

Raja replied, "Coming, mom." and then he approached us wearing pink pajamas and a yellow kurta with a green tie.

Maybe he got ready for a TikTok video, not a wedding.

Impressed with himself, as he always is, he said, "Am I looking dashing or what?"

Looking at this circus monkey, Monu whispered to me, "Why don't they make him the servant? He looks like that more than I do, right?" I smiled and was about to comment on his unique look, but his mom was as confused as me about his appearance and asked, "Raja, why are you wearing a tie on top of the kurta, and what color combination is this?"

"Fashion, mom, fashion. First, I thought I should wear a suit..."

"Then what? Granny wore it?" Monu asked jokingly.

His remark made me laugh, but it angered Raja's parents.

"I meant blazer, shirt, and trousers…"

"That combination won't look good on granny." Monu said, mocking him again.

"Monu, you go wait outside." Raja's dad responded.

"But there is no waiting machine outside." Monu retorted.

"You come with me; I will show you the machine." His dad said, looking annoyed.

As they both left, Raja commented, "This servant is getting stupider each day." Then he turned to me and asked, "Am I looking good, Urvi?" His mom stared at me, awaiting my feedback.

I replied, "Umm, if you have any other options, you can change; otherwise, this is not so bad." I said, trying to be as polite as possible.

"I knew you would love the dress." Raja replied, thanking me.

I really don't know in which world he lives and what he hears. Anyways, his mom called for Isha again. "Isha, come, girl, we are getting late."

"Coming." She replied.

Then my favorite Isha came, looking extremely hot in her pink saree. I stood up and said, "Wow, you are looking so beautiful."

Shockingly, she ignored my compliment and said to her mom, "Come on, mom, let's go." I was really angry at her for ignoring my compliment, but God knows my anger at her never lasted.

Raja's dad drove us to the wedding hall, and soon we reached there. At the entrance, 'Suhani weds Saajid' was beautifully written. As we entered, I saw my parents waiting for us, and we all greeted each other. I hugged my mom and shook hands with my dad.

Then we met Suhani and Saajid, clicked some photographs, and after having some snacks like kababs, pakodas, and golgappas, it was time to hit the dance floor. Most of us, including some known and unknown family members, started dancing, except for Raja's mom, my dad, and Isha (The introvert trio). Even granny and Monu were dancing, but not with each other, obviously. Although I would have loved to watch that. My mom is a great dancer. She danced with me and Raja's dad, who according to him is a great singer and dancer. My mom and his dad looked so good together as we danced.

I approached Isha, asking her to dance, but she declined, engrossed in her juice. To spice up the night, I struck a deal with the waiter, ensuring the next rounds of her drinks were laced with plenty of alcohol.

Then, for the sake of my parents, I danced a little with Raja. His TikTok moves were getting me all confused about what to do next. In the middle of our dance, he came near to kiss me, but I didn't let him, pointing at my dad that he wouldn't like it, and he stopped. Thanks to my dad's angry look for saving me that day.

Later, something amazing happened. Fueled by the alcoholic drinks, Isha danced with my family and then even with me. Surprisingly, alcohol seemed to have a more charming effect on her than my previous attempt with the fake thief. After two joyful minutes of dancing, I said goodbye to my parents, and we headed home, exhaustion leading us straight to bed.

In the middle of the night, I woke up to the sound of Isha vomiting. I looked at the clock; it was 1:24 am.

I quickly went to her room and asked, "Isha, are you all right?"

"Yes." came Isha's voice from inside her room's bathroom.

"You don't sound fine."

"I'm fine. You go and rest." She said and then again, she vomited.
"Should I come inside?" I asked.

"No, nothing good for you to see here."

I picked up the photo album and nachos and replied, "You're right. You finish it. I'm waiting here."

"Don't mess up my room again." She warned.

Hearing her voice, I got nervous and put them down.

"It was my first-time drinking alcohol." Isha confessed.

"First time? Really? Wait, you knew it wasn't juice?"

"Yeah, I'm not stupid. The waiter told me about the deal. But I really wanted to try. Maybe I drank too much."

"No, you didn't have too much. If you had too much, you wouldn't be in your room now. You would have been in my room."

She came out of the bathroom and stared at me. I quickly said, "No no I meant in a different room, maybe with some boys."

She smiled and said, "Sorry for not responding to your compliment before."

"It's okay. I am used to your ignorance and quietness."

"By the way, you looked really pretty in that black dress." She complimented.

"You should drink more often, Isha." I suggested.

She smiled and said, "Okay, I should go to sleep now. Tomorrow is an important day at school."

"Every day is important for you. Let's talk and dance all night and you take a holiday for a change."

"Some other day, I can't take a leave."

"Why? My Hitler dad won't allow it?" I joked.

She stared at me. And I said, "Okay, okay, sorry, I am leaving."

So, I was leaving with a sad-looking face when I heard her voice, "Urvi."

I stopped and she apologized, "Sorry, it's my nature. I just don't speak that much."

"I know, but at least speak a little. See, I'm new to this house. It's uncomfortable and awkward for me sometimes. Every girl needs a female friend to talk to."

"I will try to be more open from now on."

"Thanks, that would be great."

I turned to leave when her voice stopped me again. "Urvi?"

I looked back at her and said, "Yeah?"

"Will you be my friend?"

"Really? I would love that… Will you?"

She smiled and said "Yeah… As we are friends now. Tell me one thing, was that thief one of your friends?"

"Well, actually, Isha, the thing is, see, there is my friend Sheila. So, she thought if I..." I was continuing when I realized that she had already dozed off to sleep.

Thank God she didn't have to hear the full story. As she had already realized that the thief thing was fake, I wanted to tell her that I put that 2000 rupees of hers and 1 rupee of mine in a wedding envelope and gave it to Suhani as a wedding gift with her name on it.

The next day, I woke up, went to the kitchen, and opened the fridge to get a glass of cold coffee that Monu had made for me the day before. Yeah, he also worked some days.

I went to the living room to drink it, but as I entered, I saw them all sitting together and waiting for someone.

Is it me? Did I do something wrong again?

I thought of apologizing for whatever mistake I might have done, "I am really sorry; I won't do that again." That's actually my go-to response when more than three people are staring at me for some reason.

"Wait! you won't do what again?" Raja's mom asked curiously.

"Didn't I do something wrong? Why are you all sitting together?"

"Good morning, Urvi." Raja said with a smile.

"We are just waiting for someone." Raja's mom informed.

"For who?"

"Mayank." Isha responded.

"Who is Mayank?"

Suddenly, the bell rang, and Raja's mom opened the door. It was Mayank. He entered and gave a high five to Monu, then touched the feet of Raja's dad, mom, and granny.

"You missed Suhani's wedding." Raja's mom pointed out.

"I was at work." Mayank replied.

"You keep on avoiding family members for work."

"Sorry." Mayank apologized and then kissed Isha on her cheeks.

Oh, right, he's the photo album guy."

"How are you, Isha?"

"I am good, you?"

"I missed you a lot."

"Me too."

I couldn't control myself and asked, "Hey, what's happening here?"

Then I asked again, "Are you guys brothers and sisters?" hoping they would say 'yes'.

"No, no, Urvi, Mayank is my husband. We are married." Isha replied.

Hearing that shocking and painful news, I spilt the coffee I was drinking and said, "What? Why didn't anyone tell me that before?"

Suddenly, I realized I had spilt my coffee, mostly on Monu's hair and a little on my dress. "Oh, sorry." I apologized to Monu.

"Why are you so shocked?" Raja's mom questioned.

"Actually, Isha looks so young, and no one had..."

Monu interrupted, "Are you crazy? I just shampooed my hair with L'Oreal." and he left angrily.

"Is he using my L'Oreal shampoo bottle?" Raja asked.

"No, it was both of yours since the start." His dad replied.

"Am I using the servant's shampoo?"

"Actually, the servant is using your shampoo."

"Will you guys stop talking about the shampoo?" I shouted in anger. Everyone stared at me, and I apologized, "Sorry, let me clean myself up." and I left angrily from there to my bedroom.

Is this the end of my love story with Isha? I have been avoiding thinking about this guy since I saw him in the photo album. Did I come here for nothing? Will I have no choice but to marry Raja or any other creep?

I was really depressed, and the reason for my depression, Mayank, suddenly entered my room.

"Hey, food is ready. Everyone is waiting for you." He said.

"I am not hungry." I replied.

"Are you here to marry Raja?"

No, dude. I am here to marry your wife.

"No, actually, yeah. I mean, it's not final yet."

"Oh, this house and Raja…"

"Mayank, I am a little bit busy. Can we talk later?" I interrupted.

"Okay, sure… Have we met before? Did I do something bad to you? It feels like you are angry at me for something." He replied.

"It's nothing like that. I don't even know you."

"Cool. Talk to me when you have time. It was nice to meet you."

I forced a smile and he left from there.

After that living nightmare, I went to the bar at night to drink with my best friend Sheila. Her brother Sajal was also invited but hadn't come.

"That assh***!" I shouted while drinking with Sheila and then said to the bartender, "Bring me five more."

"Let me get this straight. You left your house to have some kind of relationship with the sister of the guy you were supposed to marry without even knowing if she's straight or single." Sheila asked.

"Am I stupid?"

"Of course, who does that?"

"Well, I do because I am such a dumb b****."

"Why didn't you tell me this before? Is the Mayank guy good?"

"Yeah, he is sweet, and she is sweet." I cried and asked her, "Now how will their divorce even happen when they both are so sweet?"

"Don't worry; you will find someone else."

"I don't want anyone other than Isha."

Suddenly, her brother Sajal came over. He looked at me and said, "Hey, why so glum, chum? Let's dance, ladies."

"I'm not in the mood now." He then turned to his sister and asked "What happened to her? Did Isha find out about the fake thief thing?"

"Worse! she's married."

"Oh, that's why she looks so sad. Do you know what I do when I'm sad?" He replied.

"Waste our parents' money?" Sheila inquired.

"No, other than that; I dance." Sajal replied, then began dancing and cheered, "Come on." The party song started, and most people inside the bar joined the dance floor. Sheila urged me, but I refused. So, she danced with her brother.

After 5-10 more drinks, I too began dancing like crazy with them. In between, I was crying, and then again dancing.

While I was here dancing, drinking, and crying simultaneously, a scene was unfolding at Raja's dad's house. Everyone was sleeping when Monu heard Raja's mom calling his name. He went to her room, and she said, "Bring me a glass of water."

"Cold or hot?

"Medium."

"Medium cold or medium hot?"

"Monu, it's nighttime. Don't make me angry. Just bring the water." Raja's mom ordered.

"Okay, bringing."

"And listen, Urvi told us that she has gone for her friend's birthday party. Has she come yet?"

"Let me check."

"This house has rules. The late-night drama won't work here. Check properly. Otherwise, I'm going to her room."

"No, madam. You stay here. I'll let you know."

After the conversation, he went to my room and found it empty. "Oh, no, she hasn't come yet. She'll be in big trouble today."

So, he called me and as I checked someone calling, I stopped dancing, went outside due to the noise in the bar and answered the call, "Hello, who is this?"

"Monu here."

"Owe, Monu, were you missing your sister?"

"No, I was missing my darling."

"Stop it. What do you want?"

"What I want is a BMW and a hot chick."

“Keep dreaming, servant. I mean, what do you want now?"

“Kirti madam is looking for you. She told me she's coming to your room. And if she doesn't find you there, get ready for a big family drama tomorrow."

“Oh, shit! what should I do?”

Suddenly, Monu heard Raja's mom calling for him and coming towards my room.

"She's coming to your room."

“What? No, wait, do one thing…” I suggested.

As she entered my room, she saw someone lying in my bed with a large blanket covering the person. Assuming it was me, she spoke without realizing it was actually Monu.

"You came! I thought you were outside.” She said. Hearing her, Monu got scared and held onto the blanket tightly.

"Urvi, are you sleeping?"

Monu put the call on loudspeaker, and then I said, "Hello, hi, sorry, I was sleeping. Were you saying something?"

"Yeah, are you hungry? You didn't eat before."

"I ate at the party."

"Okay, why are you covering yourself fully with the blanket? You will have breathing problems. Don't cover your full face."

"No, it's okay.”

“It's not safe to sleep like that, Urvi." She suggested and then came near the bed to remove the blanket from the side of his head. Monu was so scared that I think he might have peed his pants. I shouted on the call, "No, wait, don't remove the blanket.”

"Why?" Raja's mom questioned.

"I didn't wear makeup. That's… that's why I am hiding."

"Oh, so that's the real reason, I have had those days." She smiled, stepping back.

"Yeah. Okay. Good night."

"Good night." She replied and finally left the room.

"Thanks a lot, Monu. You saved me again." I said with a sigh.

"This was the last time. I won't save you again. Start behaving properly."

I thought that he had helped me so many times, so why not give him a gift, right? So, I said, "You don't have to call me sister ever."

"Really?"

"Yes."

"If you ever need my help, I will always save you."

"Yeah, you must keep on doing that. Bye." I replied and ended the call.

That poor guy doesn't know that I am a lesbian.

CHAPTER 6: BIG REVEAL

I stepped back into the bar, and approached Sheila and Sajal, and said, "Hey guys, I'm leaving."

"Why so early? It's just 1 am." Sajal commented.

"Come on, Urvi. Please stay. You came after so many days." Sheila said, convincing me.

"Actually, I've decided to leave their house tomorrow morning. So, I have to wake up early."

"Why? What about Isha?" Sheila asked.

"Sheila, I came to that house for Isha, but she's already married. That means nothing between us will ever happen. It's over for us now."

The next morning, while others were sleeping, Monu was helping me pack my stuff in the suitcase.

"Thanks, Monu, for waking up so early." I said.

"It's fine, but please don't go. Without you, this house will be so boring." Monu pleaded.

"I have to. Actually, I came here for something, but it's not possible.

"Yeah, I know you deserve someone way better than Raja sir."

I smiled, "Well, yeah."

"Even if you marry someone else, will you ever visit us?" He asked.

"I might not come to this house again, but I will definitely meet you."

"Promise?"

"Promise."

So, we finished packing.

"Finally, it's done."

"Will you leave without telling anyone?" He asked.

"No, no, I have to tell them; otherwise, my dad won't let me inside his house."

"Should I wake them up?"

"No, it's fine, they'll wake up on their own. Isha used to wake up by now, but as her husband has come, she must be busy."

Then I came near him and whispered, "Her husband must be busy with her, right?"

Monu laughed and asked, "Who? Mayank Sir?"

"Yeah, why are you laughing?"

"You think Mayank Sir and Isha madam are doing right now?" Monu said as he continued laughing.

"What is there to laugh about? They're both married, so they can."

Monu couldn't control his laughter as tears started streaming down his cheeks. "Mayank Sir and Isha madam? I can't. I just can't control it. Let me go and drink some water." He said, turning to leave.

"Wait!" I called out, stopping him, and asked again, "Why are you laughing? Tell me the truth."

"It's nothing. I'm just a jolly guy."

"We both know that happiness doesn't live inside you." I stated.

"I can't. They requested me not to reveal."

I gave him 500 rupees and said, "Now you can reveal, right?"

Monu took it and replied, "What are you doing? I'm an innocent, honest, hard-working servant. I'm not a cheap guy who reveals family secrets for money."

I gave him 500 rupees more and asked, "What about now?"

"Okay, it's time to reveal. Mayank sir is gay."

"What? Does Isha know that?"

"Yes."

"And she doesn't have a problem with that?"

"No.

"Why not?"

"Pay me!"

I gave him 500 rupees more and said, "Tell me now!"

"This is such a big secret, so you have to pay me 500 rupees more."

I handed Monu another 500 rupees, and he spilled the beans. "Isha madam is lesbian."

"Isha is a lesbian?" I shouted a bit too loudly.

"Shh, don't shout. If someone hears that, they will kill me." Monu interrupted.

Oh, what a relief! So, maybe there is hope for my love story with her. But, yeah, it will still be difficult.

"Who in here knows that?" I asked.

"Everyone except Kirti madam and granny.

"Hmm, so this is their secret."

"Promise me that you won't talk about this. They will literally throw me out of the house." He requested.

"I won't tell anyone, but on one condition."

"What is that?"

"Give me my 2000 rupees back! Why would I care if everyone in this house is gay or lesbian? You made such a big deal out of such a small matter."

"You looked excited at that time." Monu said with a sad face as he gave me my money back.

After that, he was about to leave, and I stopped him and said, "Wait, help me unpack the bag. I am not going anywhere."

"What happened now?"

"You were right; this house will be so boring without me, and I might even marry Raja." I declared.

"Ew!" Monu exclaimed and started unpacking my stuff.

The next day, I went to SLM School where my dad was the principal, and most importantly, Isha taught there. As I walked around with a flower bouquet in my hand, searching for Isha, I accidentally ran into my dad.

"Good morning, dad." I said, joining my hands in an Indian namaste style to show respect.

"Are you having back pain?" He asked.

"No." I replied.

"Then touch my feet."

"Oh, sorry." I touched his feet to show some forced respect.

"Why did you bring the flowers?"

"Actually..."

He took them from me and said, "Thanks. How are you?"

"I am fine. How is mom?"

"You didn't ask if I am fine or not."

“Are you fine?"

"Stop it! Your mom is doing good. Did you like Raja and his family?"

"Yeah, they're nice. By the way, dad, do you know where Isha is?"

"Why would I know where she is? I'm a principal, not a security guard.” He replied and left angrily.

Thanks, dad, for the sweet talk.

After my dad left, I approached a teacher and asked, "Hi, do you know where Isha Kukreja might be?"

"Yes. Go to the first floor, third room to the right. You will find her there."

"Okay, thanks." I reached there and saw Isha inside the classroom. One of Isha's students, Shamsher, was observing her from the outside, saying, "Oh God, what wouldn't I do to get her in my life?"

"Me too.” I said.

He looked at me and asked, "What?"

"What? Go to the classroom and study, and stop with your weird fantasies. She is sold!" I said, and we both entered inside.

I approached Isha and greeted her, “Hi, Isha.”

“Hey, you here?”

“Yeah, actually I came to meet my dad, so I thought why not meet you too.”

“Thanks, Urvi, for taking your time to meet me.”

“Well, you deserve a visit. Can I sit? I want to see you teach.”

“Oh, ok, sure.”

There were about 15 students in the classroom at that time. She picked up the science book from her purse and started the class, “Today we will be doing the next chapter, Reproduction."

Interesting. I came here at the right time.

Believe me or not, maybe some of the kids in the classroom had phones, but minutes after she announced the chapter name, a group of 10 more students entered the classroom. I am not even sure if they were from the same class or even school. Even Isha was shocked by their sudden entry, but as polite and sweet Isha is, she just began teaching, starting from the intro and all, and then skipping to what I remember her saying, “So, in this system, the female contributes an X chromosome, and the male contributes either an X or a Y chromosome. Hormone levels in the male parent affect the sex ratio…”

"Ma'am, I have a question.” Shamsher said as he raised his hand.

"Yes, please ask."

He stood up and added, “Actually, the last chapter that you taught us about plants, I understood that really well."

"Good.”

"The reason was that you taught with a demo by bringing some plants… why not do the same with this chapter?" He suggested with a smile.

Everyone in the classroom started laughing. Isha felt a bit uneasy and unsure how to respond. So, it was time for me to defend her, and I shouted, "Hey, demo guy, did you bring your phone?"

"No.” He replied.

"Go home and bring it here. Your browsing history will become the demo for all the students.” I said with a smile. With embarrassment, Shamsher sat down, muttering, "No demo needed."

Everyone laughed again in the classroom, even Isha did this time, feeling happy that I was there to support her.

After the school drama, I went to get the usual medicines and sweets combo for granny, and soon brought it to her room. She was really angry with me as I had gone for the medicine but instead went to the school first.

"Where did you go? You have been out since morning. Were you waiting for my death?" She asked.

"Sorry, granny, I went to the school.”

“You haven't finished your studies yet?"

"No, I meant I went to see my dad and Isha.”

“Yeah, keep on doing this family meeting nonsense and ignoring me.”

“Just take the medicines, granny. And you know what, today I brought motichoor laddu for you."

"Laddu? Why? Am I getting married or something?”

“If you don't want that, then I will have it.” I said as I took the laddu box and held it.

“I didn't mean that. Give me." She snatched it from me and added, "Why are you wasting your days meeting dads and sisters? You are a young girl. Find a nice boy for yourself."

"I came here to marry a guy, remember?”

“Who, Sonujeet? He's too old for you."

"No, no, I meant Raja."

"Yeah, yeah, I was just joking… but you don't even spend time with him. What don't you like in my handsome Raja? He's just perfect."

He is perfect? Really, granny? I mean I can write a full book on why I don't like him. Check the medicines, granny. Their side effects must be making you say stupid things like Raja is perfect.

"Yeah, I know." I replied.

"Yesterday he was complaining about you, saying that you don't talk to him. I told him that it was his fault. He's the one spending all his day doing jobs and TikToks."

"You tell him, granny!"

"You tell him, granny." She said, mimicking me in a taunting voice and added, "You also make some efforts. Go, see his company someday. They will be shooting a new ad for their AC soon. Help them so they don't make another stupid ad."

"Sure, I will."

"Okay, now go. It's time for me to sleep." I was about to leave when her voice stopped me, "Wait. Switch on the Joota sheel AC, and play a religious song on it." I smiled and switched on the AC, saying, "JC, play 'Ganesh God Prayer by Amitabh Bachchan."

"Aww, Amitabh Bachchan, my favourite." She said with a smile and slept peacefully.

As I left, I came across Mayank's room and saw him packing his clothes.

"You're leaving already?" I asked him.

"Hey, yeah.There's an important company meeting."

"Company work or something else?"

"What do you mean?"

"No, I meant how do you live so long without Isha?"

"Oh, I miss her so damn much. Yeah, life is really insufferable for me sometimes. But you know, I have to earn more and more money to give Isha the best life possible. What more can I even do?”

"You can have a baby with her. It's been so long since you guys married." I suggested.

"Baby? Yeah, baby. Babies rock. Right? ... I really want to have one, but Isha is not sure. She thinks a baby might affect her figure."

“Cut the crap. I know you are gay!”

"What? Who told you?" He said as he closed the door from inside.

“Men don't wait for years to have a baby with a hottie like Isha. I saw how you kiss and hug her. It tells about your sexuality.”

"So, Monu told you, right?"

"Yeah, but in his defense, I had to pay him a lot to reveal this."

"How much?"

“2000 rupees.”

“That's a lot for him. I would have expected him to sell out for just 500... but even if I am gay, why are you ignoring me since I came here? You have really been rude to me.”

"Oh, I am moody."

"No, it's not that. I have been noticing you.”

“What do you mean?”

“Tell me, where did you go today?"

"School, to meet my dad.”

“Dad or Isha?"

“Isha also teaches there?" I asked, looking shocked.

Mayank smiled and said, "You like her, right?"

“What? No! I like dudes.”

“Oh really?”

“I am telling you, Mayank, I went to meet my dad.”

“I saw you leaving with a flower bouquet.”

“Yeah, for my dad.”

“We both know how much you love your dad. The minute she told you about the marriage, you spilt the coffee on Monu's hair, you got all rude to me, then you paid Monu money to reveal my sexuality, and now that you know that I am gay, you are being nice to me and talking to me so politely.”

"What? No. It's nothing like that, Sherlock!"

“You just called her hottie in front of me!”

“Yeah, she is hot.”

“So, you’re telling me that you came here to marry Raja. Really?”

“Oh! That looks even worse. … okay, fine, I like Isha. Maybe I love her."

“I knew it, and I can even help you with that.”

"How, really?"

“I don't know if you know this, but Isha is a lesbian.”

"I knew that."

“Monu revealed that too. That bastard!”

“By the way, are there any other gays or lesbians in this family?"

“No, I mean none that I know of. But my point is, that Isha is a shy girl. She will take way too long to fully open up. It will be next to impossible for you to impress her in just a few days.”

"So, what should I do?”

“Do you have any other options for marriage?”

“I have Raja."

“Oh.”

“Yup.”

“Oh!”

“Yup!”

“Don't worry. I will do something. See, sometimes love takes years to happen. But some love stories even happen in a day. Tomorrow will be the beginning of your love story. Tomorrow, you will both date.” He said with a smile.

"Is that just a dialogue or will it really happen?” I asked.

“Till now, it was just a dialogue. But tomorrow, it will happen." He reassured me.

CHAPTER 7: DEATH OF MARIA

At night, I was talking to my best friend Sheila on the phone.

"Yeah, Sheila, I'm telling you, Mayank's like the best husband ever. I mean, it's really hard to find a guy who will help you steal his wife, right? I'm just so happy."

I was so happy that something might have cursed me. As Raja entered my room and asked, "Can I come inside?"

"I was just so happy." I said to my friend on the call and then added, "Wait, Sheila, I will call you later." I ended the call and answered him, "Yeah, you are already inside, so tell me."

He sat next to me on my bed and questioned, "Just tell me the truth. Do you like me?"

"What happened?"

"See, I know that there might be max to max 1% chance that you don't like me. But I just want to be sure."

"Max to max 1% chance. Really?"

"Urvi, we both know something."

"And what is that?"

"Let's be honest, Urvi. I am like a gift to humanity, right? Only some people get this gift. And the thing with the gift is, you don't return a gift, especially when it's so good. So, I am asking you again, do you like me or not?"

"Raja, you are just like a gift. A gift that I want to return." I laughed and apologized, "I'm sorry, I was just joking."

"I know, and you're funny."

"Thanks."

“You love me, right?”

“You're funny too.”

“Thanks.” He said that and stood up to leave.

But before leaving, he added, “Good night, Urvi.”

“Good night, Raja.”

“Take care.”

“You too.”

“Miss me.”

“I will try.”

“If you get bored, call me or just come to my room.”

“You go, I will surely come.” I said sarcastically.

Raja smiled and left. As soon as he left, I locked my room door and laughed. I was about to call Sheila again, but I received a call from Monu.

"Urvi madam?"

“Yes?”

"I think Raja sir is cheating on you. He told me to bring a condom. He said that a girl is coming to his room."

That creep!

"No problem, bring him." I responded.

"You don't mind?"

"Nah!"

"OMG, you are so cool!"

"I know. Bye.” I replied and ended the call.

The next morning, I woke up, and within minutes, Isha entered my room, holding a plate of food. "Good morning, here's your breakfast." She offered.

“What, why?” I asked.

“To eat.” She replied with a smile and sat next to me on my bed.

Good things don't happen to me this easily, so I stared at her and questioned, “Isha?” still wondering if it was really her or if I drank too much last night.

"Will you go out with me today?" She inquired.

I touched her to confirm the reality.

“Isha?” I repeated.

"I am not going to school today; you wanted to have some girl time with me, so let's do that today!” She said. Then she stood up and added, “So I'll be in my room. Let me know when you're ready." and she left with a smile.

“Isha?” I questioned again, still unsure WTF was happening.

I knew there was only one person who could tell me what was really going on here. So, I called her husband, Mayank. At the time, he was at the airport, probably using Grindr on his laptop. After a few rings, he answered, "Hello, Urvi. What's up?"

"Mayank, what the hell have you done to Isha?”

"I didn't do anything to her. I am gay, remember?"

"Yeah, I mean, did you just convince her to go out with me, or did you change the girl?"

"Well, actually, I told her something. Listen carefully. You had a pet named Maria."

"What? I never had a pet."

"Just listen to me. Yesterday, your cat went out for a walk, and a fast-moving car hit her. She died, with hardly anything left to bury."

“Come on!”

“You two were like the closest. So, your family members are a bit scared to give you the bad news. I requested her to keep you busy and happy all day before sharing the bad news."

"Are you out of your mind? This might be the dumbest plan I have ever heard.”

"Believe me, it will work. Isha gets much sweeter to a person who just lost someone."

“Yeah, well, I can see that. So, my dog's name is Maria?” I asked.

"Maria is your cat's name, not your dog's name."

"Yeah, dog, cat, they both are basically the same thing. If you ignore the bark and meow."

"You think bark and meow are the only differences between a dog and a cat?"

"Whatever, and you couldn’t think of a better plan than this stupid nonsense?" I said and then mimicked his voice in a taunting way – "Isha, her cat died. Go hang out with her. She will be so happy.”

"If you have a better plan, then tell her I was lying and just ask her out." He suggested.

As he said that, I thought of a better plan… to ask out a shy, introverted, married, secretly lesbian sister of the brother that I was supposed to marry. Then I realized that I was in a fuc*** up situation, and there was no better plan than this that I could think of.

"I can't ask her out on a date normally." I said to him. "Why not?" He asked. "Because I am so sad my cat died yesterday." I replied with a smile and then added, “Thanks. Bye, Mayank."

Soon, I got dressed up and ready, and Isha and I were on our way to a destination she hadn't revealed. She was driving, with me in the passenger seat, staring at her. As she noticed my stare, she asked, "Do you want to say something?"

"Nope. Yeah. Nope. No. I mean, yeah.” I stammered nervously and then I asked, "Where are we going?"

"You'll know in some time."

"Okay. Why are you being so friendly with me today?" I inquired.

"We just became friends, so I thought, why not spend a day with my new friend.” She replied.

I expressed doubt, "I don't believe you. You won't take a work leave just for me. I think you're kidnapping me."

"What if I were?” Isha teased.

“Well, I would still love that.” I replied.

"You are crazy!” Isha remarked with a smile.

"Yeah!"

We reached the destination and it was the Iskcon Temple.

“I thought we were going to see a movie or something.” I said.

"There we will go after this. Believe me, you will like this way more than the movie.” Isha reassured.

We stepped out of the car, and she held my hand and said, "Urvi, if there's anything causing you pain or sadness, or anything that might trouble you in the future, this place will help you fight that. It has helped me so many times..."

To be honest, when she held my hand, I almost stopped listening to her and just imagining my life with her.

Inside, the temple was crowded, and decorated with beautiful sculptures. We prayed in front of the grand portrait of Goddess Lakshmi.

Isha came near me and said, "Whatever you want, just close your eyes, ask, and you'll get it."

"Can I touch what I want?" I asked her, but there was too much noise, so she couldn't hear me properly and asked, "What?"

I closed my eyes, touched her, and replied, “Nothing.”

After the temple, we went to watch the latest Shahrukh Khan movie. We each had our own popcorns and cokes. I intentionally threw my popcorn, pretending it fell by mistake, and we ended up sharing the same popcorn like a couple. It was lovely, but I thought, why not make it even lovelier, right? So, I threw my straw, hoping she'd share hers with me too.

“Oh! It fell accidentally.” I said, looking at her straw.

She stared at me, then smiled, pulled out an extra straw from her purse, and gave it to me. Yeah, my plan failed!

As we left the mall after the movie, it suddenly started raining. Isha took out an umbrella from her purse and we shared the umbrella for a few seconds, but then I stepped out to dance in the rain.

"Isha, come join me!" I waved, but she declined as usual. An old lady saw me dancing and joined in, so I had to dance with her. Isha smiled at the sight.

Later, we went to an open-air restaurant for dinner and the waiter approached and asked, "Hi, can I have your order please?"

"Yes, for me, one plate tandoori chicken, half plate chilli chowmein, 2 butter naan, and a Coke or Frooti, whichever you have. That’s it. I want to keep it light for now.” I said.

He wrote it all down and then turned to Isha, "Ma'am, yours?"

"I'll have a veggie salad and a diet coke."

"Me too, bring the same for me." I quickly added.

"But you wanted so much before." He pointed out.

"Yeah, Pack that." I replied.

"Okay, thanks." The waiter said and left.

"If you want to have non-veg, then it's fine with me. I don't mind." Isha said.

"No, you are a vegetarian. So, I realized it's not right."

"As you wish."

"By the way, thanks for today. You really made my day."

"Thanks to you too. It's been so long since I went out with a friend. I just hope that you didn't get bored with me."

"No, it's always fun to be with you, Isha. Why don't we go out again tomorrow? Or this weekend?"

"It might be difficult."

"Why? Please." I requested.

"Sorry, actually I want to tell you something."

"Yes, say."

"Today, I just tried my best to keep you as happy as I possibly could because I have bad news to share with you."

"What bad news?"

"You know your cat."

"My favourite Maria?"

“Your cat's name was Maria?”

“It still is."

“Sorry, It's not anymore.”

"Did she change the name? That is such bad news. I loved Maria's name.”

“No, I meant Maria is no more. She died yesterday."

I pretended to be sad and said, “Why? How?”

“A truck hit her yesterday when she was walking alone."

“Oh no, why didn't my parents tell me this?”

“They were scared as you two were so close. Also at this time, you need someone to physically support you as you're not living with them. So, I decided…I am really sorry, Urvi."

At that time, the waiter was standing there with our food and listening to us.

"I really need a hug." I said, looking emotional.

Suddenly, he came towards me to hug me. I stopped him and said, "Not from you, creep. Just give us the food."

He served us and left. As he left, Isha came near me. I stood up, and she hugged me tightly for about 15 seconds.

"You feeling okay?" She asked.

"I am now… listen, I have to go to the washroom." I said.

"Should I come with you?"

Why not?

"No, it's okay. I'll find."

I approached the waiter and inquired, "Hey, where is the washroom?"

"Let me show you. Come with me." He offered.

"Just tell me the direction. Don't act smart."

"Sorry…walk straight and then left."

"Okay. Go now. And stop trying to impress girls."

"Sorry." He replied.

Impressing girls is my business.

You must be wondering why I missed the golden opportunity of going to the washroom with Isha. Actually, I didn't go there to pee and all. I went to dance out of happiness as I was tired of pretending to be sad, and the day surprisingly turned out to be amazing.

After some time, I came back, and Isha asked, "Are you feeling better now?"

"Yes, a little." I replied.

We both sat and suddenly we saw firecrackers in the sky. It was looking so beautiful.

"Did you arrange this?" I asked.

"No, Mayank did… this whole thing was his idea."

Yeah, I know, that dude is a genius.

"Is this my Maria burning in the sky?" I asked, looking like I was about to cry.

"No, no, they are just crackers. Not Maria."

"Not Maria!" I said and started fake crying to get some more attention from Isha and then added, "Sorry. I didn't mean to cry again."

She picked up her chair and sat near me to calm me down and said, "Don't worry. Everything will be all right. Maria must be missing you so much in heaven. Just stay calm. I am here with you."

"Thanks, Isha. You really are the best."

Suddenly, my phone started ringing, and I checked; it was an unknown number, so I rejected it. But I had received so many calls from that same number before also.

Who is it and why do I keep getting calls from this number? It's spoiling my date.

In Raja's dad's house, it was actually Raja who was calling me. He was inside the house with his parents, granny, and Monu. As a highly egoistic guy, he can't just admit that I was rejecting his calls. So, he pretended in front of them that he was talking to me.

"Hey Urvi, how are you, sweetie? Me? I'm handsome as usual. Hahaha. Oh, you're missing me again? Me too! By the way, where have you been since the morning? Oh, so you're with Isha. Okay, you should have at least told me that, darling. You called me before? Yeah, yeah, I remember now that I received like 5-6 of your missed calls. Yeah, I was busy, so couldn't pick up. Okay, you guys enjoy there. No, no, you don't have to bring me a rose flower again. Okay, baby, love you too. No, you end the call. No, you end!"

"For how long will you be doing this stupid drama? ... the phone call never even started, and you are talking about who should end the call." Monu said.

"Shut up, Monu."

"Is everything all right, son? Where is she?" His dad asked.

"She is in a restaurant with Isha. She called me before, but I was busy at that time." Raja informed. Maybe he used to track Isha's phone and that's how he got the information.

"Raja, tell us the truth. What's really going on? Do you like her?" His mom questioned.

“Yeah, mom, there is no problem.”

“And does she also like you? I haven't seen you together that much recently."

"We won't be doing romance in front of you, mom. Just chill, like our AC. Everything is fine… I need to take care of a little something in my room. Excuse me." Raja said as he was leaving from there.

"At least finish your dinner, Raja.” Granny requested.

"I will, after some time." Raja replied and went to his room.

“There must be something wrong. He always licks everything left on his plate, and today he has not even finished the food.” Granny remarked.

Actually, Raja was really sad that day because of my constant ignorance and rudeness towards him. When he went to his room, he realized shockingly for the first time that I might not like him and could possibly reject him. So, he was crying in his room silently. How do I know about this? You ask. Monu peeked at him through the door and informed me later. Even he felt bad for Raja at that time.

CHAPTER 8: NEW ADS. NEW PROBLEMS.

Some days later, Raja and his dad started making a new Just Chill AC ad, this time even stupider than before. The set was a gym. Monu played the role of a gym trainer, and Raja played himself, the fat guy. Although Raja's casting was perfect, I was confused why they had hired their skinny, no-muscle servant for the gym trainer role.

The ad began with Raja running on the treadmill. He was sweaty and tired after doing that for 5-10 seconds. So, he stopped and exclaimed, "OMG, this is too much. I'm exhausted."

The gym trainer, Monu, approached him and asked, "Hey, why did you stop?"

"I can't do it anymore. Slimming is not my cup of tea."

"Don't give up now. Keep trying!"

"I'm not feeling motivated, dude."

"Should I play a motivational song?"

"Yeah." Raja replied, and then the trainer Monu played a motivational song on the Bluetooth speaker, but he turned off the AC.

Listening to the song, Raja started running on the treadmill again but realized that the AC was off.

"Trainer, why did you switch off the AC?"

"Sorry, let me turn it back on." Monu replied and turned on the AC while surprisingly Raja was still running on the treadmill, but now Monu switched off the music.

Raja got angry at his trainer and asked, "What are you doing? Why can't you keep both the AC and music on?"

"Sir, the electricity bill has been coming so high these days. If only there was a thing that could play music and cool the room at the same time, that would solve all our problems."

Suddenly, Raja's dad entered the gym wearing a magician's costume, a shiny black dress, and a black hat. He carried a loudspeaker in his hand and spoke into it, "Install Just Chill AC today and feel the change. Just Chill AC..."

Me and Isha were at the set secretly watching the ad, but I couldn't tolerate it anymore, so I came in front of the camera and shouted, "Stop it, please, just stop!"

Raja, his dad, and Monu stopped acting. They were shocked to see me there.

"Urvi, you here? Were you watching the ad?" Raja asked.

"Yes, I was."

"Did you like it?"

"I am sorry."

"Okay, but did you like it or not?"

"I said I am sorry… Don't you know what that means?"

"She didn't like it, son." His dad stated.

"Oh." Raja replied, in shock.

"You surprised us with your entry. You should have told us. We would have sent the driver to pick you up." His dad said.

"That wasn't necessary. Actually, I wasn't able to spend that much time with you guys recently, so I thought why not surprise you with a visit."

"Thanks, Urvi, for coming."

"Also, I have an idea for the AC ad." I said with a smile.

“But we already have the script and everything ready.”

“Yes, but my idea is really good”

“See Urvi, you can't just make an ad. Ad-making is a complex process. Leave it to us, the professionals.” Raja replied.

"At least we should listen to her.” His dad said to Raja and then looked at me and added, "Urvi, tell us your idea."

"Actually, it's not just an idea. I have come prepared… There is a girls' college nearby where I did my bachelor's, and Isha and I will be performing this new ad in the canteen area there."

“Isha?” His dad asked curiously.

“She’s here. I have been trying to convince her for this ad for days, and finally, she agreed."

Isha came there, and I asked, “Are you ready, Isha?” Isha nodded, “Yes.” and we went to the location with a camera and stuff. It was so nice seeing my old college. The special thing this time was that I came with Isha. I wished she was in my college too. That’s why I thought of an ad that had both of us as friends, and I wanted to capture this moment. So, even if things didn't work out between us, I would still have a memory of us together.

The ad began with Isha sitting in the college canteen area and looking all stressed up. I came, sat next to her and said, “Hey, Shiela is having a party tonight at a club. You coming?”

“Nope.”

“Why? What happened… Did your boyfriend leave you?”

“Yup.” Isha replied, looking tense.

I came near her and put my arm around Isha's shoulder. “But your girlfriend hasn't.” Isha stayed quiet, and I added, “Come on, don't get too heated up.”

“Bro, switch on the AC.” I said to the canteen guy, played by Monu.

Monu, the canteen guy, switched on the Just Chill AC, and within a few seconds, I asked her, “Now, are you feeling cool?”

“The room is, but my mood is not.” She replied.

"JC, play a happy song.” I said, and as JC played a pop song, the camera focused on Isha in a close-up shot, where she closed her eyes, soaking in the coolness entering her body and mind.

And I asked her again, “How is your mood now?”

“I am good. Why are you asking?”

“Your boyfriend left you. Remember?”

Isha smiled and replied, “Which boyfriend?”

I looked at the camera and said, “Get Just Chill AC for your home right now. Just say it. Play it. Chill with the Just Chill AC.”

“It's time for a cool change.” Isha added.

We both laughed, and the ad ended.

Everyone in my college watched the ad live, and as it ended, they all clapped. Isha and I approached Raja and his dad for feedback.

“It was amazing. I loved the tagline.” His dad appreciated.

“Beginner's luck, it wasn't that bad.” Raja said.

Actually, the last two ideas of the Just Chill AC ad were his, so he was jealous. I glared at him, and he changed his statement, “Okay. It was good.”

We went to the Just Chill company office, and after editing and stuff, in the meeting room, we showed the office staff this ad, and they all loved it. I approached Isha, and we both talked in whispers.

“Thanks for helping me, Isha.”

“We are friends now, so you don't have to thank me anymore.”

I smiled, and suddenly, Raja took my hand and led me to the center to introduce me to the office staff, “Hey, everyone, this is Urvi Khurana.” They all greeted me, and then he added, “She's not just a good ad maker, but she also has a good choice of men. Yeah, she’s my fiancée.” Everyone clapped and cheered in the room. In excitement, Raja came closer to kiss me on my cheeks, but I avoided it, instead looked in a different direction, and smiled, “Sorry, I have to go.”

Raja and his dad were really disappointed in me for ignoring that kiss, and Isha was confused. Although I loved doing these things to Raja, I didn't know why, but I regretted it that time.

I thought, *It was just a kiss on my cheeks. I should have let that happen.* But on second thought, I concluded, *Nah, I did it right. My cheeks deserve better lips. Also, I didn't bring sanitizer, face wash, or soap.*

Still, I went to his office room to talk about it.

"Can I come in?" I asked.

"If you want to.” Raja said, looking a bit pissed off.

"Come on, why are you angry at me? I am not your fiancée; we had a 30-day deal before I tell you about my decision."

“You don't need 30 days; you have already made up your mind to reject me. Although yeah, it's shocking and even unbelievable that a girl doesn't like me because girls die for me.”

“Raja, you know how many girls like you in real. Why do you keep showing off? Just admit the truth."

"Yeah, okay I know, I just say these things to make myself happy. To tell you the truth, Urvi, I thought girls like handsome and rich guys, and I am both, right?"

"You are right about the rich part."

"Anyways, but the fact is, no girl has really liked me. No girl!"

"That's not true. Granny likes you."

"There is no girl left in her."

"No, I meant, it's not like that. You are a nice person, even if not, then also you are a rich guy, and that's good. I am not saying I don't like you, but..."

"But you are not saying that you like me either."

"Yeah, but…"

"Listen, Urvi, I just have one request from you. Already two girls have rejected me for marriage, and that's the reason my family is not really happy with me. They think I am getting rejections because of my nature, because everyone knows there is nothing wrong with my looks. As I look dashing, right?"

I stayed quiet as it felt like he was about to cry.

"If you don't like me, that's fine, it's shocking but it's fine. Whatever decision you make at the end of the month, that day, say anything, just don't insult me in front of my family." He said and started crying.

I felt like hugging him, but there was just too much of his body to hug. I wasn't sure if one person could do that. So instead, I put one of my hands on his shoulder and said, "Don't cry, you will find someone you deserve, even if it isn't me, you will still have someone, I am sure. And I won't insult you; you don't have to worry about that."

"Thanks, Urvi, for understanding... and listen, why not make a TikTok to celebrate this big conversation between us."

"You force me to insult you." I warned him.

"Sorry, by the way, why did you decide to talk to me today?"

"Monu told me that you were crying in your room when I was having dinner with your sister Isha."

"He saw me?"

"Yeah."

"Oh! And you don't have to say, your sister Isha, she's the sister of both of us."

"What? No! What? Just shut up!"

Suddenly, I received a call from my bestie, Sheila. I picked it up and said, "Hi, Sheila… oh, today? ... yeah, I love night outs… is this even a question to ask me? ... just tell me the time."

"Can I also come?" Raja asked.

"No!"

"Please, you know I am sad, and I even cried in front of you. I deserve to go." Raja requested.

"Can Raja come? ... No? ... Why not?"

"Tell her that I am rich." Raja suggested.

"He is saying that he will pay for our drinks and food."

"Tell the rich part!"

"Also, he is loaded… yeah, with money… yes… okay, so now you agree? You money-minded girl!"

"You are going with us." I said to him.

"Yippie! Thanks, I just love my money."

We both went to the bar. It was shocking that I entered my happiest place intentionally with Raja. Anyways, we met Sheila and her brother, Sajal, and danced and enjoyed ourselves. As Sheila was fond of rich guys, no matter what, so she danced with Raja.

Sajal found a girl who liked him, and he danced with her. I danced alone but still had a lot of fun, especially when Raja fainted after a few drinks with Sheila. We left him lying on the floor, and Sajal left with the girl he was dancing with. Just Sheila and I remained, and I wanted to do something crazy that day, like getting a tattoo. Well, not as many as Sheila; both her arms were fully covered with them.

"You know what, Sheila? You've been asking me to get a tattoo. Let's do it today!"

"Really? What kind of a tattoo?" She asked.

The next morning, I was in bed when I heard Monu knocking on my door. "Urvi madam, can I come in?" I ignored him and searched for my phone to check the time. While doing so, I noticed a tattoo of Isha's name on my right inner forearm. "Oh, shit!" I shouted a little bit loudly. Monu heard me and said, "Urvi madam, what happened? Can I come inside?"

"No, no, wait."

"Why?"

"Just wait a minute. I am busy." I was wearing a sleeveless top, but to cover my tattoo, I started looking for a full-sleeve in my almirah.

"Is there a man in your room that you are busy hiding?" Monu asked. Fortunately, my mother had packed one for me in case I got sick.

I wore it quickly and replied to him. "Are you crazy? I came to this house to get a man in my life."

"Yeah, and that too, Raja sir." He said mockingly, in a lowered voice.

"I can hear you!"

"Sorry."

So, I wore it, but it felt unbearably hot due to the high temperature that day. I couldn't even turn on the AC because that would make them suspicious of my sickness.

"Come in." I said.

Monu entered the room, eyeing me suspiciously, and started searching for any sign of a man who might have left through the window or been hiding.

"There wasn't a man in this room." I clarified.

"It's hard to believe, but okay… why are you wearing this big dress in such hot weather?"

I pretended to sneeze and showcased my fake sickness, "I am not feeling well."

"Why didn't you tell me before? I would have brought a medicine for you."

"Really? You work here?" I teased.

"Don't joke."

"Bring me now."

"I will. Do you have a fever?"

"Kind of."

"Cough?"

"No."

"Cold?"

"Yes."

"Diabetes?

"What does diabetes have to do with a cold? Just bring me the medicine." I shouted.

"Okay, okay. I am bringing."

After he left I unfolded my sleeves, and checked the Isha tattoo. *What did I do? Why did I do this last night?*

I found a sketch pen in my purse and added "war" after Isha, trying to make it Ishwar. Ishwar is a hindi word that means God. Although it became Ishawar, I still thought it might be enough to fool others if someone saw it. I looked above and prayed to God, "This tattoo is for you, please save me." Suddenly, my tattoo knocked on the door. No, I meant Isha. I quickly unfolded the sleeves and babbled nervously, "Yeah, who? Why? Yeah. Sure. Come in."

"Hey, are you feeling sick. Monu just told me."

"Yeah, a little bit."

"Oh, don't worry, he's just bringing the medicine."

"I hope he is… are you going to school?"

"Yeah, I'm not really in the mood to go. Especially on Mondays, I never feel like going."

"Why don't you wear 'I Hate Mondays' T-shirt to school?"

"No, I am afraid other teachers might also be wearing that… Also, on Mondays, no one really wants to study. As I start writing on the blackboard, they open their lunch boxes to eat. And you know what? They've come up with a lot of dirty nicknames for us."

"Really? What's yours?" I asked.

"I will tell you someday."

"I will be waiting for that day. Anyways, I am happy that hanging out with me has taught you to talk."

"I knew talking just wasn't comfortable with you before." Suddenly, her phone's alarm bell rang. "Oh, I am getting late. Talk to you later. Take care. Bye."

"You too." I replied, and she left.

She's so perfect.

And then Raja came in my room and asked, "Can I come inside?"

"I don't think you can come any further."

"Sorry. Bad habit… Monu just told me that you are sick."

"Just told you? Hasn't he left yet?"

"No, he doesn't go like that. First, he will tell everyone in the house. Then, he will wait for you to die. After that, he goes to buy the medicines. That's his standard process."

I smiled, and he continued, "Don't worry, I will send him in a minute."

"Thanks."

"If you want, I can take a leave and take care of you."

"No, it's not necessary. I will be fine."

"Oh, I just realized you don't want me to stay with you so your cold doesn't spread to me because you love me so much, right?"

"It's not like that, but you can be positive and keep thinking that."

"It is that. Take care. Bye." Raja said and left.

I closed the door to look for a solution to this tattoo problem as I was feeling so hot wearing those full sleeves.

Suddenly, Raja's dad and mom knocked on my door.

Why do they keep coming one by one?

“Come in, come in." I said, and they both entered.

"Do you have cold? Monu just told us about it.” Raja’s dad said.

“He hasn't left already; let me bring the medicine myself."

"No, no, you rest. After telling granny, he might just leave.”

"Okay, I'll be fine. It's just a minor cold. You guys don't have to worry. Monu unnecessarily made a big deal out of it."

"Oh, you are fine? So, Monu made me miss my lady cheater show for nothing? I'm going back." Raja’s mom said and left the room to continue watching the show.

"Take care, Urvi. I'm also getting late for the office. Meet you at dinner, okay?"

"Sure." I replied.

Then, at dinner time, we all sat down to eat, except granny, who stood near the dining table, visibly upset. Isha and I were sitting together, discussing our day.

"Pass me the curd, please." Raja’s dad requested, and his wife handed him the curd.

"Granny, sit down." Raja urged, looking at her.

"I won't be sitting down today. I have seen enough!" Granny exclaimed.

"Are your hips hurting again?" Raja inquired curiously.

"What? No!"

"What happened, mom?” Raja’s dad questioned.

"What happened? You people have gone blind, but my eyes are still sharper than ever. They see everything. They understand everything." Granny said angrily, and then shouted, "Urvi, stand up!"

I stood up and asked, "What's wrong, granny?"

"First of all, stop calling me granny. Everyone who enters this house calls me granny. Even electricians and plumbers call me granny. I have a name."

“Sorry.” I apologized.

Maybe here, too, I should start referring to her as Raja’s granny and not just 'granny’.

“It took me sometime but I know everything now. I know your purpose for coming to this house. You were never interested in Raja, right? You came here for someone else!”

“Mom, what are you saying?” Raja’s mom questioned.

“Let me talk!” Raja’s granny shouted.

I looked at Isha, feeling terrified. I wondered if Raja’s granny knew about my feelings for Isha. Maybe Mayank had told her.

"All this time, you both spent with each other, laughing and calling. Do you both think I am stupid?" Raja’s granny continued.

Isha also thought that she was talking about me and her, as we had been spending a lot of time together. She quickly clarified, “No, granny, it's not…”

"Isha, you keep quiet." Raja’s granny interrupted.

"Granny, gran, aunt, Raja's granny, me and Isha are just…" I babbled.

"Keep quiet and show me your right hand."

I was scared as hell. *How did she find out about my tattoo? What is happening here?*

CHAPTER 9: DEEPIKA IS SO HOT

"Sorry, but when did you see…?" I began to say and was about to show them the Isha tattoo when Raja's granny interrupted, "I saw it when you were using this right hand to put a bandage on Monu's finger."

"What? Monu?" I asked.

"What?" Isha said.

"Yes, I know everything that is going on between you and Monu." Raja's granny stated.

Then I realized what actually happened and why she must be thinking that Monu and I were having an affair.

Before, when Monu and I were talking and I was shouting "What does diabetes have to do with a cold? Just bring me the medicines." and before he left, saying, "Okay, okay, I am bringing."

At that time, Raja's mom was passing by my room. I was feeling so hot in that sweat machine full sleeves dress. I thought, instead of covering my whole body just to hide a tattoo, why not hide it with some bandages.

So, I asked her where I could find the bandages, and she said they are in the medical cabinet in her husband's room.

They have a medical cabinet, and still no cold medicine?

But before I could go there, she told me to bathe first with hot water as it will help with my sickness. I wondered why she was so obsessed with me bathing. I mean, who tells a sick person to bathe?

I listened to her and went to bathe, and after doing that, I realized that I forgot to bring my towel. I opened the bathroom door and peeked into my room, but it wasn't there. I stepped out of it into my room naked. Luckily, no one saw me, and I closed the door from inside.

I was about to wear my summer clothes, Monu knocked on my door and said, "The chemist sold, I brought medicine for your cold. Open the door, have the disease no more."

I extended my non-tattoo left hand outside the door to take the medicine. "Just give it to me.” I said and he gave and asked, "Why are you not opening the door? Are you hiding a man again?" Why did he think of me as a slut? "I am not hiding a man; there was no towel in my bathroom, so I am changing the dress. Now, leave!"

As he left, he came across Raja’s granny, who asked him where I was, and that intelligent creep, Monu said, "I was just talking to her, she is in her room naked; don't go now!" Yeah, so that was the first thing that made her suspicious.

After putting on my clothes, I was heading to Raja's dad's room to get the bandages, making sure to cover up my right hand with the tattoo. But near his room was Monu's room, and I just wanted to check what he was hiding because he looked like a thief to me. At that time, he was busy watching an Amitabh Bachchan movie with Raja’s granny. So, I decided to enter his room.

I imagined his room would look like a public bathroom with photos of female celebrities stuck on the wall, some DVDs with the name ‘homework’ but surprisingly, as I entered, it was super clean. Maybe I was the dirtiest in this house, as my room was always messed up. Anyways, there were some photo frames of Monu with a decent looking woman, which I thought was his girlfriend or someone he had kidnapped.

Other than that, some usual cleaning stuff that you expect in a servant's room. I was about to leave his room when I found something amazing. Yeah! A cheap wine bottle. So, obviously, I opened it and drank, and soon I felt dizzy and fainted on the floor.

Sometime later, Raja's granny passed by his room and saw me lying there. Well, that was her second suspicion. But she also noticed my Ishawar tattoo and remarked, "Oh! I didn't know she believed in God, but she should definitely learn the spellings."

Later that evening, when Monu was making dinner in the kitchen, he accidentally cut his finger and screamed, "Aaah! It hurts, it hurts." I regained consciousness at the sound of his voice, entered the kitchen, and saw that Monu had hurt his finger.

I finally went to Raja's dad's room to get the bandages. First, I put some on my tattoo. After that, I went back to the kitchen and put a bandage on Monu's finger.

He looked at the bandages on my arm and asked, “What happened?” “Oh! I donated blood yesterday.” "LOL, you donated blood! You must have fallen while running away from Raja sir." “Yeah, you’re right.” Then. I started helping Monu with dinner; we joked around, comparing Raja's belly to watermelons and eggs, and laughed together. Little did we know, Raja’s granny was watching everything.

Now, let's put a stop to the flashbacks and continue with the story.

“I am having an affair with Urvi madam?” Monu said and then whispered to himself, “Good for me.”

"Are you asking or confirming?" Raja’s granny questioned.

"I am already married.” Monu informed.

"To Urvi? You married her already?" Raja’s granny inquired, raising an eyebrow.

"No, no.” Monu shouted and showed us his marriage photos on his phone. "See, this is my wife."

"What?" We all asked him in unison.

"When did you marry?" Raja’s dad asked.

“Didn't you guys know that I was married?”

"You're a servant, not Salman Khan, for whom we search on Google every day for the marriage news." Raja responded.

"And mom, don't say things like Monu and Urvi!” Raja’s mom exclaimed.

“You think about me in this way, Raja's granny? This is really shocking. Now never ask me to bring your medicines and sweets combo.” I retorted.

"Sorry, Urvi. I am old. Those medicines are playing with my mind.” Raja’s granny replied.

In anger, I left from there and locked my room door.

"Granny, why did you insult her like that? Please stop thinking of yourself as Sherlock Holmes. I have told you many times.” Raja commented.

“It's not my fault. Times have changed. Nowadays, it's tough to understand what is romance and what isn't.” Raja’s granny stated before leaving for her room.

In my room, I was lying in my bed, angry at Raja's granny for thinking that I would rather have an affair with Monu than Isha or Raja. Then there was a knock at my door. It was Raja and his parents.

"Urvi, are you all right? We are extremely sorry. Please forgive granny.” Raja’s dad apologized.

“These things happen. The same thing happened in one of the shows I watched last night.” Raja’s mom remarked.

"I am not angry, just want to get some rest. The pills I took are making me all sleepy. Don't worry, I will talk to you guys tomorrow."

"Please talk to me in case of any problem.” Raja said.

"Sure."

“Or come to my room.”

“I will.”

“You didn’t come last time.”

“Raja!... stop it.” His mom yelled at him and they all left.

I started using my phone, looking at a selfie I took with Isha, and suddenly I received a call from her.

"Hey, all fine? You looked really angry.” Isha said.

"Yeah, yeah, don't worry.”

“Granny crossed all the lines today, right?"

"She did. Actually…"

"I thought she was talking about us." We both said at the same time.

"Really?" Isha asked.

“What?” I said.

"No, nothing. Okay, then…”

"Yeah, let's sleep. Talk to you tomorrow?"

"Sure, good night, Urvi.”

“Good night, Isha."

So, our call ended, but what I came to hear from Mayank was that as soon as she was done talking with me, she called him.

He answered the call, “Hi Isha, what's up?”

“Were you sleeping?'"

"Kinda. How are you?”

“If you are tired, we can talk tomorrow."

"Come on, Isha, I am your husband, even if the fake one, but you can talk to me at any time."

"How is Deepak?"

"He has just gone to sleep."

"Listen, I want to tell you something."

"Yes. Please tell."

"I'm in love."

"What? Really? Who's the lucky girl?"

"I don't know how to say this."

"Is it Urvi?"

"What? No!"

"Is it?"

"Yeah."

"Nice choice."

"It's not a nice choice, Mayank. She's straight and she's here to marry my brother. What should I do?"

"Do you think she likes you too?"

"Sometimes it feels like that. The way she talks to me and believe me, she spends way more time with me than my brother."

"Then maybe it could work. See, nowadays everything can happen. Love has no boundaries. Just stay positive. You've always made the right decision, Isha. There's so much to like in you. Trust your feelings."

"Thanks, Mayank. I always feel better when I talk to you."

"And I'm happy that you're cheating on me." Mayank joked.

"Haha! Stop joking. Good night."

“Good night, Isha.”

As soon as he hung up his call with Isha, he called me, and I answered, "What happened, Mayank? So late?"

"Yeah, sorry for calling at this time, but I have great news for you.”

"What’s that?"

“Isha loves you."

"What?” I shouted, in shock.

Suddenly, I saw a rainbow outside in the sky. My Isha tattoo started glowing, and I was jumping up and down in my bed, waving the lesbian flag and crying with happiness.

Yeah, none of these things actually happened, but I was really happy.

"Isha just called me and said she loves you, but she's worried because she thinks you're straight, and that you're here to marry her brother."

"Why does she think that I want to marry her brother? Oh, yeah, I just realized. You didn't tell her anything, right?"

"No, I didn't.”

"So, I just have to prove to her that I'm a lesbian, and she'll be mine. That's so easy!"

"It won’t be that..."

"Okay, bye, Mayank."

The next morning, I woke up, went to the kitchen, and saw Monu making tea while singing his own-made tea song about it.

"Hot, hot tea, you must drink. Even if you don't know how to make it, then also, you must drink. Hot, hot tea, you must drink."

I entered the kitchen to request him to stop with his crappy song. "Can't you just play music on your phone or on the AC rather than singing this nightmarish song in the morning?"

"This song is good, and so is my voice."

"Don't sing this stupidity outside your bathroom."

"Okay, sorry."

"Anyways, what are you making?"

"Tea."

"But, I don't drink tea."

"So?

"So, this is tea!"

"Who said it's for you? I am making it for myself."

"What happened to the cold coffee? I thought you would be making it for me daily."

"No, that was a one-time thing."

"Have some shame. You are not doing a government job that you are not afraid of getting fired."

"There are worse people than me in this house."

"That's a good point."

"Why did you wake up so early today?"

"I couldn't sleep, good news kept me up all night."

"A proposal from a handsome man?" He asked.

"No, not from a man. You shut up!"

"Okay. Okay. Don't tell.... Listen, I am going to the bathroom. Turn off the gas after one minute and put the tea in my cup." He replied and left.

Thanks, servant, for giving me the chore.

I checked his cup. It had Monu's name imprinted on it.

This servant is crazy as hell!

Suddenly, Isha came there and said, "Hey."

"Hey, what, yeah, who, hi, hello, good morning."

"I don't really know what used to happen to me, but back then, almost every time she greeted me or came near me, I got so nervous."

Did I say every greeting word possible?

Isha yawned, looking sleepy, and said, "Good morning, Urvi."

"Didn't you get much sleep last night?"

"Yeah, I was thinking about someone." Isha replied.

"Who?" I asked, with a smirk, hoping she would say my name.

"No, no, not someone. I meant something. Yeah, normal school stuff, homework and all."

"Yeah, sure." I said sarcastically.

She looked at my arm and asked, "Wait! why the bandages?

"Oh, this? I donated blood yesterday."

"Really? You?"

Why doesn't anyone believe that?

"Yeah." I replied.

She stared at me suspiciously and asked, "What are you doing here?"

"Just making tea." I responded as I switched off the gas.

"For me?" Isha asked.

"You? ... yeah, obviously." I replied, poured the tea into a nice cup and gave it to her.

"Thanks, Urvi." She expressed, and went with me to the living room to drink it. She added, "Listen, I want to talk to you about something."

"Really?… you sit here, I am coming in a minute. Okay?"

"Sure."

As she started drinking the tea and reading the morning newspaper, I went to the kitchen, and inside it, I looked for what to do about Monu's tea. As I didn't really know how to make tea, I opened the fridge and took a 500 ml full cream milk pouch out of it. I poured enough to fill Monu's cup, threw the rest of the milk in the dustbin, added five to ten spoons of Tata tea, and mixed it with a spoon. After that, I went to talk to Isha.

She pushed down the newspaper and appreciated, "Urvi, this tea is so good."

"Thanks. I always make the best tea." I replied proudly.

"Do you want to go somewhere today evening?"

"Yeah, sure. What's the occasion?"

"You made such a nice tea for me. I should at least take you out somewhere. Also, tomorrow you will be making your decision. So, before that, I want to go with you."

"Sure, anywhere you want."

"Thanks."

Then I remembered Mayank's words, "She loves you, but she's worried because she thinks you're straight, and that you're here to marry her brother."

So, I decided to drop some hints that I'm into girls. I picked up the newspaper and pointed at a picture of Ranveer Singh and Deepika Padukone advertising for a brand and said, “I just love this couple. They look so good, right?"

"Yeah.”

“You know what? I like Deepika more than Ranveer Singh. She's so hot, right?"

"Yes, she is. But I thought you'd be more into Ranveer. Don't you think he's hot?"

"No, I prefer Deepika. Only Deepika!"

Monu, who was overhearing us, holding his Monu-imprinted cup, commented, “Who doesn't like Deepika? She's super hot." Then he took a sip and exclaimed, "What the hell is this?”

In the kitchen, Raja’s mom was busy packing lunchboxes for Raja and his dad who were whispering about me.

"It will either be your best day or another nightmare.” Raja’s dad remarked.

"What do you mean by another nightmare? Are you talking about my previous two rejections?" Raja asked.

"Yeah, obviously. To tell you the truth, I don't think there are many chances of a yes."

"She will say yes, dad. If she wanted to say no, she would have run away by now."

"But there could be a twist in the end."

Raja’s mom was observing their conversation and interrupted, "What are you, dad and son, whispering about?”

“Urvi… tomorrow she will tell us the decision."

"Yes, I know."

"She will say yes. Don't worry, guys." Raja reassured.

"Want to make this interesting?" Raja's dad asked.

"Sure, how much?"

"I will pay you 10,000 rupees if she says yes, otherwise you have to pay me."

"Done."

"Don't you guys have any shame left? Betting on something this serious?" Raja's mom remarked.

"Sorry." Raja and his dad apologized.

"You know, a similar thing happened in one of the shows I watched. Count me in your bet, I bet 10,000 rupees on her saying no." Raja's mom said and left from there.

In my room, I was talking to my mother on the phone.

"Till now, I haven't even decided what to say, mom… you know me… actually I like his..."

Suddenly, I heard Raja's granny shouting my name, "Urvi, Urvi, come here"

"Coming."

"Come fast!"

"Someone is calling me, talk to you later, mom."

I ended the call and rushed to Raja's granny room and saw her and Monu watching TV together.

"Oh, you missed it." Raja's granny said.

"What?"

“We just saw your Just Chill ad with Isha sister.” Monu remarked.

"Really? No problem. Call me the next time it comes."

"I will.” Monu replied with a smile.

"No, you won't.” Raja’s granny warned him.

I smiled, and was leaving from there when I heard her voice stopping me.

"Urvi, listen."

"Yeah?"

"Why don't you make one ad with Raja too?"

"Maybe later."

"When? After marrying him?"

“Umm... I don't know. I have to go." I said and left the room but stood outside the door to overhear their conversation.

Monu laughed and said, "You will lose the bet. I am telling you, she will say no!”

“Hmm. I might have to give you 500 rupees tomorrow. I had so many expectations from Raja."

In the evening, Isha was driving the car with me in the passenger seat.

"At least tell me where we are going.” I requested.

"It's a surprise.”

"Are we going to another temple?"

"Not a temple."

"Thank god!" I exclaimed, and she glared at me.

So, I changed the topic.

"Isha, tell me something."

"Yeah?"

"If a boy loves a girl and wants to propose, but is afraid of rejection, should he propose?"

"It depends on the chances of acceptance."

"There is, like, a 10% chance."

"Then one must take this much risk for their love… even if the chances are 1%, then also one should propose. If they can think of a future together, then they shouldn't hesitate, just go for it. There are far too many risks in the world, but too few love stories."

We reached our destination, and to my delight, it was my favorite place – the Bar.

"OMG! Bar!" I said with excitement as we both stepped out of the car.

"Raja told me that you like coming here. I thought why not spend some time with you at your favorite place."

"Thanks, Isha. You're the best."

"Come on, let's go."

We entered the bar, and to our surprise, a local male celebrity singer was also there. Isha and I greeted him, and he agreed to take a selfie with us. Then, he grabbed the mic and sang a romantic dance song from a popular Bollywood movie. We danced, drank, and had a lot of fun. As the song was about to end, I kissed Isha on the lips in front of everyone in the bar. She was completely shocked and left the bar quietly without saying a thing.

CHAPTER 10: HAPPILY, EVER AFTER?

Outside the bar, I followed Isha and shouted, "Isha, wait!" and she stopped.

"What happened?" I asked.

"Why did you kiss me in front of everyone? You came to our house for my brother, right?"

"That was all a drama, Isha. I don't like Raja or, for that matter, any other man. The day I met him, I wanted to reject him. But you came. And I fell in love with you. I love you, Isha."

Isha was stunned and replied, "I don't know how to react."

"You can react by saying I love you too." I said, then removed my bandages and showed her the Isha tattoo, "See, I didn't really donate, I got a tattoo of your name."

"What? Why did you do that?"

"This is nothing. And why are you looking so shocked? I know that you love me too. Mayank told me everything yesterday. Then why are you scared to say it back? I am just like you, Isha. I am attracted to girls." I reassured her.

"He told you?"

"Yes! You love me, right?"

"I do, Urvi. But what will you say to my family or even your family? How will this even work?"

"We don't have to explain anyone, Isha. We will run away tomorrow."

"What?"

I bent down on my knees.

"Urvi, wait! what are you doing?" She asked.

“Isha, will you marry me?”

“Urvi…I…”

I took out a ring box from my purse and opened it. To her surprise, there wasn't any ring inside but two Goa tickets.

"What's this?"

"I don't have a ring now. That I will give you in Goa. Will you escape with me tomorrow?"

"Are you crazy? No, I can’t leave my family for you." She responded.

"You can't run away with me, but you can marry a gay person!”

"Urvi, listen." She held me and made me stand up and then added "We haven't known each other enough. It's been less than a month. But do I have feelings for you? Yes. Do I love you? Yes. But I won't leave my family and run away like that. It’s not practical. Sorry, I won't do it.”

“Isha, but they would never accept us.”

“Without their acceptance, I won’t go anywhere.”

"You know what, Isha? You are a coward! You are so afraid to show your real identity to other people that you even married a gay man whom you hardly talk to. But you can't be with someone you truly love. For how long will you keep hiding yourself from the world just for the sake of your family?"

"Urvi, I just can't do it. And please, don’t think about leaving your family for something that might never happen.” Isha said, turning away to leave.

I called her name repeatedly, "Isha, Isha, please come back!" But she didn't stop or look back at me. I sat on the corner of the road and cried.

After a few hours, I entered the house and found Raja waiting for me. He looked all dressed up, perhaps wanting to take me somewhere. He waved, said hi, and extended his hand to give me a bouquet of flowers.

"Urvi, do you want to go with me?"

"Please leave me alone. I'm not in the mood." I replied and left.

He pleaded, "Urvi, Urvi, please just listen." but I didn't stop and entered my room, locking the door from inside. I didn't want to hurt him, but Isha's rejection had affected me deeply.

Later at night, I decided to go to Raja's room to explain my situation. But as I approached his room, I peeked through the door, and he seemed tense. His parents were there, trying to comfort him.

"Don't worry, Raja. Urvi isn't the last girl. There are so many more girls we know of, even better ones, who will make you happy. Even if she says no, you will still have more options." Raja's mom reassured him.

I went back to my room, lied in bed and pondered my next move. Soon, I packed my bag, and decided to leave the house in the middle of the night when everyone was asleep. I couldn't say no to Raja, and a relationship with Isha seemed impossible.

If I had told my dad the real reason for coming to this house and revealed my sexuality, he would have scolded me or maybe grounded me. Perhaps he would have forced me into marrying someone like Raja. I didn't want any of that. The only choice I could think of at that moment was to escape, go alone to Goa, and perhaps start a new life there. Yeah, I knew that I would miss my mom and Isha, but at that time I didn't really know what else to do.

Before leaving their house, I went to Isha's room where she was asleep peacefully. I wanted to hug her but was afraid of waking her up. Instead, I placed the ring box with her Goa ticket and the 10rs selfie printout inside one of the drawers on her bedside table, blew her a flying kiss, and left the house with my suitcase.

The next morning, as I sat bored at the airport, things weren't as dull at Raja's house. Thinking it was my final day, Monu brought a cup of coffee to my room for the first time. But, he didn't need to knock this time because my room door was already open.

He entered and was shocked to see none of my belongings; the room was empty of the things I brought. He understood I had left the house. He rushed to the living room and shouted, “She left! Urvi madam left!”

Everyone except granny woke up and gathered there.

“What happened, Monu?” Raja’s mom asked.

“She's gone. There's none of her stuff in her room.”

Isha was also there but remained silent.

“When did she go?” Raja’s dad inquired.

"How would I know? I didn't tell her to go… let me call her.”

“Yeah, you do that” Raja replied.

Monu went outside to look for me and call me, but I didn't answer his calls. Raja’s granny entered there, annoyed, and said, “What's happening? Why are you all shouting so much in the morning?"

"Granny, Urvi ran away.” Raja informed.

“With whom?” Raja’s granny questioned.

“We're not sure." Raja’s dad clarified.

“Where is Monu?"

"He is outside… we already told you, there’s nothing going on between them." Raja’s dad replied.

Isha went to my room to find a clue or something that I might have left, and then to her room where she found the ring box and the selfie printout in one of the drawers. Realizing that I was at the airport, she put the ring box in her purse, ignored the selfie printout and and started changing her dress.

Meanwhile, in the living room, everyone was furious at me for leaving abruptly.

"Call her parents. She needs to answer for her behaviour. We treated her well, and she did this to us." Raja's mom said.

"I am calling them. This is outrageous behaviour." Raja's dad stated angrily.

Monu entered the house after a few minutes and said, "She's not picking up the phone."

"I talked to her parents. They are coming here." Raja's dad informed.

"Let me call the police. Someone must have kidnapped her; otherwise, she would have been here and said yes to me." Raja declared.

"So, you think, the kidnapper took her belongings too?" Monu asked.

"Yes, obviously."

"Son, are you done making yourself feel better?" Raja's dad questioned.

"It's not that; I am calling the police; you will see…"

Isha overheard Raja, rushed to the living room and pleaded, "No, no, no, don't call the police. I know where she is. I will bring her here. Don't worry, please."

"Let me also go with you." Raja said.

"You stay right here. If she had liked you even a little bit, then she wouldn't have left like that. So, if you go with Isha, then she's never coming back." Raja's granny intervened.

“You are right, granny.” Monu agreed and Isha left the house.

Raja sat down on the chair and cried. He was really embarrassed and expressed, “I requested just one thing from her. Say no, but don't insult me in front of everyone. Yet she still insulted me."

"Don't cry, son. If you want to do something, then pay me my 10,000 rupees of the bet.” His dad said.

Raja was taken aback, "What?"

Raja’s mom chimed in, "And my 10,000."

Raja was puzzled, "What is happening here? You guys are still thinking about your winnings of the bet?”

“We called her parents. Isha is finding her. Monu is mocking you. What more can we do other than get our bet money?" His dad responded.

"But she hadn't said no.” Raja insisted.

"She ran away from the house; that's a no in capital letters.” Raja’s dad retorted.

"But she can come back and still say yes, right?" Raja, still hopeful, questioned.

"You are so positive, son. Don't be this positive. And just give us our money.” Raja’s dad advised.

"Okay, okay.” Raja agreed and sent 10,000 rupees each to his parents’ bank account through a UPI app.

"Granny, grannies, my 500 pennies.” Monu requested.

"I am not giving anything. You earn like 500 rupees a day working here. Take a leave tomorrow.”

"That's not fair… I should have betted with Raja sir." Monu replied angrily.

It was 12:45 pm, and the flight was scheduled for 2:30 pm. So, I was engaging myself with a movie on my laptop when suddenly I noticed Isha approaching. Shocked and excited, I wondered, *Is it really happening? Has she left her family for me?*

"Isha, I can't believe you chose me.”

"No, I didn't. I came to bring you back.” Isha replied.

“Oh!”

"What the hell, Urvi? You left without even saying a word to anyone. My family was so nice to you. We never did anything bad to you, Urvi. You could have said no, but you rather embarrassed my brother and my family and ran away.” Isha expressed her frustration.

"I didn't run, Isha. I booked an Uber.” I joked.

"Really? Even at this time, you are thinking of jokes? And where will you go, leaving your family like this? Will you leave me too?" Isha inquired.

"I wanted you to come with me. You are the one who's letting me go. Because you are scared of your family.”

"I am not scared of my family. I love them, and I don't leave those I love. That's why I came here, to bring you back.” Isha stated.

“Well, I am not going back now."

"You don't leave your old relations for new ones, Urvi. Both are equally important. Please don't leave. Come with me. We will talk to them. They will understand.” Isha pleaded.

"They won't understand, Isha, and you know it.”

“I will reveal my true self. Happy? I will tell them that I love you and you love me. Just don't go, please.” Isha urged.

"It won't work.” I said.

"Don't give up on us, Urvi." Isha requested.

"I don't want to but I am really scared of going back."

Isha understood my situation and said, "Give me your laptop."

"Why?"

"Just give it." She insisted.

I handed her the laptop, and she sat down next to me and opened Skype. "Let's do a video call and try here. If everything's fine, then you are going back with me. All right?"

"Yeah, video call is better. At least no one would be able to slap me." I remarked.

While Isha started logging into her Skype account, discussions were ongoing between my and Raja's family. They all were angry at me. Yeah, like they usually were!

"With whom was she yesterday?" My mom asked.

"Isha." Monu replied.

"What was she doing with Isha? She should have been with Raja. Where were you, Raja?" My dad questioned.

"He was crying in his room." Monu answered.

"Shut up, Monu!" Raja retorted.

"Urvi didn't even eat food yesterday." Raja's mom mentioned.

"Even Isha didn't eat much." Raja's dad added.

"That potato dish that this Monu servant made was tasteless. I have told him many times to put salt in food. But he never listens. I don't know what he is doing with all the salt. Maybe he is selling it to make some extra money." Raja's granny remarked.

"Yeah right. I am selling loose salt on the streets." Monu said angrily.

Suddenly, Raja received a Skype call on his laptop and said, "Wait guys, I am receiving a video call from Isha."

He accepted the call and put the laptop in front of everyone to see.

"Hello, Urvi, Isha. Where are you both?" Raja asked.

"I found her at the airport." Isha replied.

"Why are you leaving the city when I'm here?"

"Or country." Monu added.

"Shut up, Monu!" Raja exclaimed.

"It could be an international flight." Raja's granny chimed in.

"What nonsense is this, Urvi? Without even informing anyone, you left their house and went to the airport? Come here right now. I will scold you so badly today. You will be grounded for an entire year!" My dad shouted.

"If you say it like that, she will never come." Monu commented.

"Urvi, why are you doing this? Where are you going?" My mom asked.

"I am running away, mom." I replied.

"But it looks like you are sitting." Raja's granny observed.

"No, I meant I am leaving Delhi."

"Why are you leaving? You didn't even tell us if you like me or not." Raja said.

"She ran away. What more hint do you need?" His dad remarked.

"But why did you leave? What wrong did we do to you? This thing I have never seen in any of my serials." Raja's mom said.

"I ran away because I know you people won't understand me or my situation. I don't like Raja."

“That was obvious. We all knew that. This thing you could have said here openly. We wouldn't have minded that.” Monu commented.

"I would have.” Raja replied.

"I love someone else.” I declared.

"So, you should have told us that. Who's that boy, Urvi?" Raja’s dad asked.

"Is it Monu?" Raja’s granny inquired.

"Granny, stop it with Urvi and Monu. They are not a thing.” Raja’s mom said angrily.

"Also, I am married.” Monu added.

"No one believes that.” Raja’s dad retorted.

"Who do you love, Urvi? Tell me. Who could be better than me?" Raja questioned.

"She loves me.” Isha revealed.

“What? My sister?” Raja questioned.

“Isha, are you drunk?" Raja’s mom asked.

"What? No.” Isha replied.

“What the hell are you saying? My daughter is attracted to men, only men.” My dad exclaimed.

"No, dad. Yeah, I was confused in the beginning. But since I saw Isha, it has become so simple to me. I like Isha, dad. I am a lesbian."

"What is a lesbian?” Raja’s granny asked.

“It’s the lady's version of gay?” Monu answered.

“What is gay?" Raja’s granny asked again.

"Stop it, Urvi. This can't be true.” My dad shouted.

"Dad, I love Isha, and she loves me. I want to marry her, but she won't do it without the acceptance of our families." I explained.

"What's happening here? I don't understand anything." Raja said.

"It's not new for you to not understand anything." Monu teased.

"Urvi, Isha, have you both gone mad? Nowadays, anyone's marrying anyone. What is happening in this world? How will you both have babies? Learn something from Amitabh Bachchan. He married a woman, and they have kids. A man should marry only a woman. That's what Amitabh Bachchan taught us." Raja's granny remarked.

"Please don't drag Amitabh Bachchan into this?" Raja's dad requested.

"Granny, we both love each other. And that's all that matters. Our hearts fall in love with a person, not a gender. Love is blind." Isha stated.

"But those blind couples are always a man and a woman." My dad retorted.

"Who said that, dad?" I asked.

"I don't understand this girl-girl thing. Someone explain to me." Raja's granny inquired.

"Let me explain, granny. Usually, a man likes a woman, and a woman likes a man, right?" Monu said.

"Yes." Raja's granny replied.

"So, they are straight because they are moving in a straight direction, as per society. But if a man likes a man, he is gay. And if a woman likes a woman, she is a lesbian. And if a man or a woman likes both a man or a woman, then they are bisexual."

"I like both Raja and Isha. Am I a bisexual?" Raja's granny questioned.

"What? No, no." Monu said.

"Stop explaining this to her." Raja's dad shouted.

"Isha, you are already married to Mayank. What are you doing?" Her mom asked.

"Mayank is gay." I clarified.

"What does gay mean?" Raja's granny inquired.

"He likes a man." Monu explained.

"I like Amitabh Bachchan. So, am I gay?"

"No, no, mom. Please stop talking!" Raja's dad requested.

"But then why did he marry you?" Raja's mom asked.

"That was all a drama. I knew Mayank was gay and about Mayank and Isha. I wanted to tell you, but…" Raja's dad revealed.

"You knew Mayank is gay and Isha is a lesbian?" Raja's mom asked.

"Yeah." Raja's dad replied.

"Oh my God!" Raja's mom exclaimed.

"I am sorry, Kirti. I really wanted to tell you, but…"

"What the hell is happening here? My head is exploding." Raja exclaimed.

"Play music on your Joota Sheel AC. Your mood will be back to normal." Raja's granny advised.

"I also knew that Urvi is a lesbian." My mom revealed.

"What? Why didn't you tell me that?" My dad questioned.

"I am sorry but I didn't know how to explain it to you." My mom apologized.

"Dad, I told mom not to tell you this." I clarified.

"Urvi, you don't talk to me." My dad warned.

"This is who she is, Kamal. She can't change that. You can't change that. If she's attracted to women, does that mean she should stay alone all her life just because society or you might not accept her?" My mom reasoned.

"Dad, I've always tried to make you happy. Usually, I fail. You have controlled me all my life and made all my decisions for me, and I accepted that. But you can't control who I am attracted to. Even I can't control that."

"Kamal, I don't know about you, but I support my daughter. If she thinks Isha can make her happy, then she has my blessings. She's a big girl. She should be able to make her own decisions now." My mom declared.

"I love you, mom." I expressed.

"Love you too, Urvi."

"Isha, I support you. Your happiness is what matters to me. If you are happy with Urvi, then I am happy with your happiness." Her dad stated.

"Thanks, dad." Isha replied.

"And I am in support of both of you. Get married and do send me all of your honeymoon pics." Monu suggested.

Listening to that, Raja's granny slapped the shit out of Monu and shouted, "Go from here, make some food, and stop asking for honeymoon photos of others. And do add salt in the food this time."

"Sorry." Monu said and left the room.

"Isha, you did really wrong this time, and the worst part is you all didn't even think that I deserved to know all this." Raja's mom said.

"It's your fault. You spend all of your days watching your stupid TV serials that you didn't even know that your daughter has married to a gay man and now she again wants to marry but this time a woman that her brother was supposed to marry." Raja's granny criticized.

“Mom, sorry, please give Urvi and me a chance.” Isha pleaded.

“Dad, please.” I added.

“Forgive me, Kirti, forgive me and Isha, there’s no point in her staying in an unhappy marriage when she has someone who will forever make her happy.” Raja’s dad said.

“You might be right. Urvi is at least better than her with a gay man.” Raja’s mom remarked.

“Is it a compliment?” I questioned.

“No, but it’s a yes from me too.” Raja’s mom replied with a smile.

"What about you, Raja’s granny? Do you accept us?" I asked.

"Oh! I don’t really care. I probably will forget about all this tomorrow."

Suddenly there was an announcement for my flight, ‘Ladies and gentlemen, this is the final boarding call for passengers traveling on flight DLX-007 to Goa. Please proceed to gate A12 immediately with your boarding passes ready for scanning. The flight is scheduled for departure shortly.”

“That’s my flight.” I said and everyone looked at my dad as he was the only one who hadn’t accepted my sexuality or my relationship with Isha.

“Now everyone has agreed to their relationship Kamal, you also please accept our daughter for who she is. One can marry a right or a wrong person, but there is no right or wrong in gender. If you force her to marry a person she doesn’t even love, she will leave us, and we both will lose our daughter forever. As parents, isn’t it our duty to keep our child happy?” My mom said.

“Urvi.” My dad uttered.

“Yes, dad?” I replied.

“You are not running away… do you really love Isha?”

"I do, dad."

"But both of you haven't known each other for long. Also, this type of marriage is not even legal in India. If in the future, you two remain as happy as you are now and same-sex marriage becomes legal here, then you both have my blessings."

"Really, dad?"

"Yes." My dad replied.

"I love you, dad."

"I love you too, Urvi. And if I was ever rude to you, I'm sorry."

"If you ever?" We all said to him.

"Come back, Urvi."

"No, no. Wait!" Raja's dad called out.

"What happened, dad?" Isha asked.

"You both are at the airport, and have the tickets, right?"

"Yeah, we do." I responded.

"So, why not go there and, Urvi, this time do a 30-day trial with the person you are really interested in." My dad suggested.

Everyone except Raja laughed, and my mom said, "Yes, Urvi. You go and enjoy with Isha."

"Thanks mom, I am okay with this. Are you, Isha?"

"But I didn't bring my clothes." Isha replied.

That's even better.

"So what? That means more shopping for us, right?" I winked.

"Okay. I am going." Isha chuckled.

"What about my marriage?" Raja said.

"You get used to staying alone." Raja's granny remarked.

"You don't have to, Raja. My friend Sheila keeps talking about you, so while Isha and I enjoy our Goa trip, why not give her a try?" I suggested.

"I will marry anyone at this point." Raja said desperately.

"I will call her and arrange your date."

"Thanks, Urvi. I hope you both enjoy your trip." Raja expressed.

Everyone gave their blessings to both of us, and we went on the trip. It was a really a good one, filled with lots of special memories. But that's the story for another time.

For now, let me share this with you. It's been five years, and a lot has changed. I achieved my dream of becoming a fashion designer. Even the guy I was supposed to marry, Raja, is happily married to my bestie, Sheila. They already have two kids, and the Just Chill AC brand is now a top AC brand. They even launched their coolers, which Raja always wanted.

For the past two years, Isha and I have been living together in our apartment. Living with her has been even more fun than I imagined. She's not a teacher anymore. Now she's the principal at the same school where my dad was before he retired.

You might be wondering why I am still calling her Isha and not my wife. Even though I thought convincing our families and Isha would be enough to marry her, the Indian legal system still doesn't allow same-sex marriage. So, my dream of marrying Isha is still on hold. I've been waiting for five years to legally marry my soulmate, but will it ever be allowed? Well, I can only wait and hope.

www.ingramcontent.com/pod-product-compliance
Ingram Content Group UK Ltd.
Pitfield, Milton Keynes, MK11 3LW, UK
UKHW061541190726
13845UKWH00031B/1147